THE MIGHTY HOOD

ERNE BRADFORD

ERNLE BRADFORD

THE MIGHTY HOOD

THE WORLD PUBLISHING COMPANY

CLEVELAND AND NEW YORK

Published by The World Publishing Company
2231 West 110th Street, Cleveland 2, Ohio

Library of Congress Catalog Card Number: 59-11532

FIRST EDITION

HC360

We that survive perchance may end our days
In some employment meriting no praise;
They have outlived this fear, and their brave ends
Will ever be an honour to their friends.

Epitaph by Phineas James, Shipmaster,
"To his stricken comrades" (1633)

CONTENTS

1. "H.M.S. Hood Will Proceed . . ." 15
2. Birth of a Ship 20
3. Her Ancestry 28
4. Mediterranean Cruise 36
5. Politicians and Others 45
6. The Sea Life 51
7. One Day in 1922 61
8. Start of the World Cruise 69
9. "Leviathans Revealed . . ." 77
10. To the New World 86
11. The Spanish War 95
12. The Guns of the Ship 104
13. North Sea, 1939 114
14. Mers-el-Kebir 122
15. Mediterranean, 1940 135
16. Watch in the North 144

17. Battleship Bismarck 149
18. Into the Arctic Circle 161
19. The Denmark Strait 167
20. Enemy in Sight 171
21. "Prepare for Action!" 180
22. Death of a Giant 187
23. Revenge 195
24. Post-Mortem 210
Envoi 220
Appendixes
A. MOVEMENTS OF H.M.S. HOOD (1920-1939) 222
B. SPECIAL SERVICE SQUADRON 226
C. THE CAPTAINS OF H.M.S. HOOD (1920-1941) 228
D. SHIPS ENGAGED IN THE BISMARCK ACTION 229
Bibliography 231
Index 233

ILLUSTRATIONS

The following illustrations appear in sequence after page 128.

1. Bow view of H.M.S. Hood (*Imperial War Museum*)
2. The most graceful ship in the world (*Imperial War Museum*)
3. At Melbourne, 1923 (*Radio Times Hulton Picture Library*)
4. Alongside, after refitting (*Radio Times Hulton Picture Library*)
5. In the Panama Canal, 1924 (*Radio Times Hulton Picture Library*)
6. 4-inch antiaircraft gun (*Radio Times Hulton Picture Library*)
7. In the Firth of Forth, 1932 (*Radio Times Hulton Picture Library*)
8. Main bridge and control position (*Imperial War Museum*)
9. At full speed (*Imperial War Museum*)

DIAGRAMS

(Based on H.M.S.O. charts by permission of the Controller of H.M.S.O. and of the Hydrographer of the Navy.)

The pursuit of the Bismarck May 23/24, 1941, p. 164

H.M.S. Hood and Prince of Wales action with Bismarck and Prinz Eugen, p. 209

ACKNOWLEDGMENTS

This history could not have been written without the help of the Record Office of the Admiralty. In particular, I am grateful to Mr. E. Hepworth and Mr. E. R. Holly for their long forbearance with my requests for records and information, dealing often with matters more than a quarter of a century old.

I would also like to acknowledge my debt to the library of the Imperial War Museum, and to Miss R. E. Coomb. In enabling me to gain a general picture of the background against which the Hood played her part for the twenty-one years of her life, her assistance was invaluable.

I am indebted to so many officers and ratings of the Royal Navy, both serving and retired, who at one time or another formed part of the Hood's company, that I can do no more than ask them to accept this general acknowledgment. Their help has been of the greatest value in providing those small details, without which any portrait is no more than a lifeless mask.

E. B.

THE MIGHTY HOOD

I

"H.M.S. Hood Will Proceed . . ."

The clank of cable coming in, its heavy thump along the decks, the flicker of a dimmed torch, or the occasional glow as a black-out screen was pushed aside—these things alone showed that a fleet was getting under way.

To the whir of winches, or the "Heave! one—two—three—HEAVE!" of men, the last boats were being hoisted on board. Funnels rumbled and emitted, for a brief moment, a roll of oily smoke as additional sprayers were switched on to the boilers. Here and there auxiliary craft, some with mail and stores, others landing or embarking personnel, lingered alongside the darkened warships. An arrowhead of foam going past, quick and hard through the pewter-colored sea, indicated a high-speed launch, with senior officers perhaps, or last-minute dispatches. It was midnight, May 21, 1941, in Scapa Flow.

The great anchorage was dark and silent save for these few signs of activity. To the north loomed Mainland, or Pomona, largest island in the Orkneys, with its capital, Kirkwall, and its memories of the Norsemen—the Temples of the Sun and Moon, and the great monolithic Stone of Odin. To the east were the quiet islands of Burray and South Ronaldsay. To the west lay Hoy with the pinnacle rock of the Old Man of Hoy standing detached from its northwest coast, guarding the entrance to the sound. Norse islands—islands destined to hold long ships ever since Harold Fairhair had added them to Norway in the ninth century—they had been the main war base of the British fleet since Admiral Jellicoe had selected Scapa Flow in preference to Cromarty Firth in 1914.

Looking at the Flow today it is difficult to remember how many ships it held then, difficult to recall this inland sea filled with destroyers, with escort vessels coming and going, and the waters of the firths scarred by the wash of cutters and many launches. The sound of the bosuns' calls no longer drowns the noise of seabirds over the headlands. In spring, though, when the islands are starred with wild flowers, and the salt sea smell is mixed with bruised grasses and herbs, it is even more hard to realize what it was like that May, eighteen years ago.

It was the long darkness when the dawn seems unimaginable. From Norway to the Atlantic coast of France an ironbound continent confronted Britain. Greece had been invaded. The battle for Crete was beginning. Everywhere the mounting losses of shipping reflected the contention that if Britian could ever be beaten, it would only be by strangling her sea lines and starving her out. The pressure was being applied now, and the screw tightened. The heavy cruiser Prinz Eugen was at sea, and with her the world's heaviest and most modern battleship, the Bismarck.

As the British ships weighed and made for the gates of Scapa Flow—the booms opening up before them and the heavy nets sliding through the water—the men with the cold, unglamorous task of protecting the great anchorage watched them go. It was a little over a year since Lieutenant Gunther Prien had penetrated Scapa Flow in the U-47 and sunk the battleship Royal Oak. He had come through a gap in the defenses of Holm Sound, noting in his log as he did so: "It is disgustingly light. The whole bay is lit up." Those weaknesses had been eliminated, but the watchers and defenders had to remember that whenever the fleet went out and the gates were open, there was always a chance of an enemy getting in.

The darkened ships slid past, silently hush-hushing through the water. The destroyers were first, moving rakish and graceful to take up their screening positions outside. Big ships were coming out too.

Dialogue varies little from one war area to another, or from one war to another for that matter.

"What's up, mate?"

"Some flap on. Fleet's going out."

"'Ope no one 'its the gate. Last time it cost us twenty-four hours solid to fix things up."

On board the destroyers there was the inevitable grousing of small ship sailors, who tend to have the same feelings about battleships as a collie dog does about its sheep.

"Always us. Only got in yesterday."

"There's a big panic on."

"They spends weeks swinging round the buoy, and as soon as they goes to sea we 'as to go too."

"They can't look after themselves."

"This'll wreck the chiefs' billiards party in their second-best saloon!"

"They're both coming out."

"They" was always the battleships to destroyer men—a sardonic "they" reserved for capital ships, aircraft carriers, and the remote figures of the senior officers and politicians who directed the war.

Both of them were coming out—the new Prince of Wales, and the old, the world-famous Hood. Their silhouettes were visible now against the lines of the sea and the islands: the long sweep of their foredecks, the banked ramparts of their guns, and the hunched shoulders of bridges and control towers.

We shall never see their like again, but no one who has ever watched them go by will forget the shudder that they raised along the spine. The big ships were somehow as moving as the pipes heard a long way off in the hills. There was always a kind of mist about them, a mist of sentiment and of power. Unlike aircraft, rockets, or nuclear bombs, they were a visible symbol of power allied with beauty—a rare combination.

Achates, Antelope, Anthony, Echo, Electra, and Icarus—the destroyers went past—their names culled from myth, legend, and history—then the new battleship, and then the ship that was almost a legend herself, the Hood.

She was 860 feet long, with a displacement of 44,600 tons, a battle cruiser designed before Jutland had been fought, and the ship that above all others had represented British sea power in the harbors and oceans of the world during the uneasy inter-war years.

In the destroyers, when they were "washing down" heavily, or when shore leave had been long in coming, or on any other occasion when the *matelot* was fed up with his lot, he would sigh for a comfortable billet in one of those leviathans that—to his way of thinking—never seemed to go to sea. His chorus was always the same:

> Roll on the Nelson, the Rodney, the Hood—
> This one-funneled basket is no mucking good!

Although they might despise battleship life and feel themselves superior sailors to the big ship men, there were times when they thought nostalgically of the comforts, the canteens, and the large messdecks of the Hood and her sisters.

The ships were all heading out now into the night and the sea. The boom gates were closing, the normal antisubmarine patrols were resuming their stations, and aboard the ships left behind, in the shore stations, and in the humble boom-defense vessels, routine went on. It was just after midnight and the watches had changed over. There were cups of cocoa in the galleys, and men were pulling off their sea boots and stockings before rolling into bunks or hammocks. The islands were pools of darkness against the glow of the northern sky, and the night wind smelled of the turf as well as the sea.

Beyond the confined waters of the Flow the destroyers were skating into position, moving on to bow and beam and quarter of the giants. Their asdic* sets were combing the dark fathoms, and their lookouts were posted. Duty watch helmsmen and telegraphists were relieving the Special Sea Dutymen who had taken the ships out of harbor, and navigating officers were putting down a last fix before leaving the shore line.

The force was bound for Hvalfiord in Iceland, there to refuel. Then, under the command of Vice-Admiral Holland in the Hood, they would proceed again to sea and cover the northern approaches to the Atlantic. Theirs was the force detailed to watch the cold, treacherous Denmark Strait.

Dropping the Seal Islands of the Orkneys behind them, the ships turned to the northwest and increased speed. Their bow waves began to crest and shine against the dark gray paint, and their sterns settled deeper as the screws took up their thrust against the sea. Directors and turrets began to turn. Voices echoed over a complexity of wires or down the simple bell mouths of bridge pipes. The sky was cloudy and the wind came from the north.

*Sonar.

2

Birth of a Ship

It was a long time since she had been built—another world almost. But it was similar in one respect—it was a world at war.

Lord Fisher had been First Sea Lord when she was laid down. From the Admiralty, his pen spluttering with indignation and the underlinings coming fast and furious on the paper, he had written to Admiral Beatty on March 5, 1915:

> I've had a big fight to get you Pakenham [to command the Second Battle-cruiser Squadron]—fierce endeavours in other directions. Pakenham is a brave man. Also Pakenham believes in you. We must have officers who believe in their Admirals instead of back-biting them. But what can you expect when Sir Gerard Noel writes to the First Sea Lord protesting against my being at the Admiralty and saying, "God help the Navy"? We have laid down 187 new ships since 15th November (four of them battle-cruisers of 33 knots and 15-inch guns) and all of them will be fighting within a year. God *is* helping the Navy.

Extravagant, eccentric, at times almost irrational, emotional—but with a genuine sincerity and patriotism unequaled—Lord Fisher comes to life in his letters.

One of the battle cruisers to which he referred was the Hood. She was not fighting within a year, but before that year was out Lord Fisher had resigned. Disagreeing with Winston Churchill, then First Lord, over the Dardanelles campaign, he had said, "I was always against it." He had also said, "This is wartime, and we can't have any damned folly about susceptibilities. Don't you worry about any odium—I will take that and love it." He retired to become Chairman of the Inventions Board, but the four battle cruisers he had written of with such gusto and affection—"33 knots and 15-inch guns"—were taking shape in the hammering shipyards. More than twenty years later, one of them, the Hood, would be at sea under war conditions and still engaged against the same German enemy.

The Hood was born in the thundering, clanging yards of John Brown & Company, on the banks of the Clyde, the "strong" river of Lanarkshire, the largest firth on the western coast—the building ground of great ships. But before a section of her keel was laid, before a rivet was driven, or the dimensions of angle bars or channels, frames, girders, or strakes specified, the design of the vessel had to be passed and approved. The naval architects who designed the Hood were guided by the overriding factor that she was to be a battle cruiser, not a battleship.

The distinction is important, and her history is meaningless without some knowledge of her ancestry. The battleship itself was a logical development of the old "line-of-battle" ships, ships capable of standing and fighting the heaviest adversary in the line. At the close of the nineteenth century, with Germany arming and with the building of the High Seas Fleet, the necessity for Britian to be able to meet a heavy threat in home waters became obvious to Admiral Fisher. The final outcome of a great deal of experiment was the Dreadnought. The first all-big-gun ship, she mounted movable turrets, three on the center line and one on each side, each turret holding twin 12-inch guns.

The race between England and Germany was now joined—the race to produce the heaviest armored, heaviest gunned battle fleet. But heavy armor, massive turrets, and the weight of the new guns inevitably meant that a loss in speed had to be accepted. Fast ships, of course, were still needed: as commerce raiders; to protect the fleet; and to act as supporters to the line-of-battle ships. These fast ships were the cruisers, some of them armored, and known as second-class cruisers; some of them unarmored, light cruisers.

But between the battleship and the cruiser lay a world of difference, and it was in an attempt to bridge this gap that the battle cruiser was evolved. The driving idea behind her conception was that she should be fast enough to cope with enemy cruisers and destroy them with her greater firepower; but at the same time she must be heavily enough gunned and sufficiently armored to be able to stand in the line of battle and, if necessary, fight against the slower but more heavily armored battleships. The battle cruiser was a hybrid and, like many hybrids, she possessed a unique beauty. She had, though, her deficiencies, in staying power and resistance—deficiencies which are also sometimes marks of the hybrid. In a footnote to *The World Crisis, 1911–14,* Winston Churchill wrote:

> Contrary to common opinion and, as many will think to the proved lessons of the war, I do not believe in the wisdom of the battle cruiser type. If it is worth while to spend far more than the price of your best battleship upon a fast heavily gunned vessel, it is better at the same time to give it the heaviest armor as well. You then have a ship which may indeed cost half as much again as a battleship, but which at any rate can do everything. To put the value of a first-class battleship into a vessel which cannot stand the pounding of a heavy action is a false policy. It is far better to spend the extra money and have what you really want. The battle cruiser, in other words, should be superseded by the fast battleship, i.e. fast strongest ship, in spite of her cost.

"She was the most beautiful ship I ever worked aboard. . . ." I was in a bar on Clydeside in November 1940, an ordinary seaman in my first ship. An old man was telling me about the Hood.

"I've seen her but once since the war," he said. "O' course she's been refitted like, over the years. But you couldna' spoil those lines. I was only an apprentice then."

It was difficult to visualize him as a young man. The ship I was in was only an armed merchant ship. (I felt a little ashamed that I was not in a real warship.) And here was a man who had helped to build the Hood. I had seen her only once myself, sliding through a gray mist off the Pentland Firth, with her escorting destroyers looking like the flunkies and outriders of royalty.

"I remember weel the day that Lady Hood launched her. As she went doon the ways I was looking at my bit of plating, just on her starboard quarter—the plating I had worked on mysel'."

Now I could see him as a young man—a handkerchief round his neck, and his eyes shining as he watched her smoke down into the sea.

"She's oot there noo," he said, with a twitch of his head toward the Firth. But she was not visible, and I knew that he meant she was somewhere out on the gray sea.

"I'm gettin' on," he said. "It's many years. She's still working, though."

He was old, and there was another war, and he was living on his pension, but something he had helped to build was still afloat and working. He had a small gleam of satisfaction on his face—like that old admiral, perhaps, who used to thrust acorns into the ground on his country walks and smile to know that one day they would make great oaks for the wooden wall of England.

It is a long time between the conception of a great ship and the moment when the workmen begin on her. After the requirements of a ship like the Hood are laid down by the naval staff, the Director of Naval Construction and his assistants must evolve the outlines or preliminary designs, balancing one requirement against another. A warship of her magnitude involves so many more factors than even the largest merchant vessel that there can be hardly any comparison between them.

There are gunnery, engineering, armor, communications, torpedo, and antitorpedo requirements—so many and so varied, in fact, that design must always remain to some extent a matter of compromise. The vessel is to be fast, but at the same time there is the gunnery school demanding the heaviest possible guns. When a solution between these two worlds has been worked out, there remains the demand that she must be able to receive an appreciable amount of underwater damage without losing her fighting efficiency. Yet this, which necessitates armor plating and "bulges," must still be achieved without detriment to her speed. Finally, something like fifteen hundred men have to be accommodated, given sleeping and eating facilities, and some space for recreation.

Unlike the ships of the German High Seas Fleet, the Hood had to be designed so that she could be lived in, and be battleworthy, in any part of the world. (It is not so difficult to build an almost unsinkable ship for engagements in the North Sea only—a ship which will have nothing but limited periods away from the comforts of barrack rooms and shore living quarters.) England with her world-wide sea communications had to produce ships that could fight from the Denmark Strait to the Pacific. In the twentieth century, the century of specialization, the warships of the Royal Navy had to be capable of specialist action and yet be Jacks-of-all-trades. Such a compromise was an uneasy one, and the Hood started with these disadvantages.

She cost £6,250,000 to build, and those were the days when the pound was truly a pound. Her contemporary, the battleship Queen Elizabeth, cost only £2,500,000. But, while the Queen Elizabeth had a displacement of 27,500 tons and a speed of 25 knots, the Hood displaced 41,200 tons and had a speed of 32.1 knots. After Jutland the weight of her armor was increased, but she still remained a battle cruiser in conception, even though her armoring was now nearly as heavy as that of a contemporary battleship. A writer in the *Naval Review* was later to point out: ". . . the extra 7 knots speed of the Hood has been obtained at the cost of some 14,000 tons additional displacement and about £2,030,000, namely 14,000 tons at £145 per ton."

So she rose up on the slipway, transverse and longitudinal watertight bulkheads; armor plate 12 inches thick on her sides; protective bulges against torpedoes, and the great keel lying rigid beneath her mounting weight; the great keel—her backbone. One hundred and five feet on the beam and 860 feet long, she was a giant among ships.

Thousands of men spent millions of hours on her construction—and most of them would never even see the finished ship. Electricians, ordnance workers, steel smelters, technicians of every sort, engineers, and torpedo artificers (for she carried six 21-inch torpedo tubes)—all over Britain men worked on their different contracts. For her, the ingots were slabbed down in the press and rolled, annealed, cooled, and straightened. For her, the steel plates were lifted into the carburizing furnaces and subjected to intense heat for two to three weeks. For her, oil and water tempered the plates—plates as large as twelve feet by ten, and weighing nearly 30 tons.

Armor plating was not new, but many technical improvements in its manufacture had occurred between 1900 and World War I. In one sense it was not new, for as early as the eleventh century Scandinavian saga-makers had sung of a ship with "its sides sheathed in iron"—"Ljot the Pale is in the east in the Swedish isles; he has a 'dragon,' covered with iron above the sea."

The Hood was heavily armored—but she had been designed before the lessons of Jutland had been fully appreciated. The effect of plunging fire on the upperdecks of capital ships meant that those decks needed to be as well protected as her flanks.

As the ordnance factories machined and proved her guns—eight 15-inch guns each weighing 100 tons and housed in 900-ton revolving turrets—her four propellers, weighing 20 tons apiece, were being cast. Meanwhile riveters, suspended like the Lilliputians over the frame of Gulliver, were busy at their noisy, skillful trade.

The very names of the rivets have a music of their own—snaphead, and countersunk, panhead, rough hammered point, snap point, and panhead with conical neck. Above, on the rapidly forming decks, some of the riveters would be heating their metal bolts, an apprentice keeping the fire at its right temperature. With a swift twist one of the men would lift the hot rivet, the tongs he used seeming like a steel extension of his arm, so easy was the movement. Beside him the bell mouth of a flexible tube gaped in the gray air. With a flick the hot rivet rattled down the echoing pipe, to leap out somewhere below, where another man seized it and, while the fire was still in the metal, thrust it into position in plate or frame.

On August 22, 1918, three months before the German High Seas Fleet steamed down the Firth of Forth to surrender under the guns of the Grand Fleet, the great hull took the water. Too late to play a part in the first of the world wars, old by the time the second one broke out, the ship that now moved slowly to the restraining hawsers of fussing tugs was to dominate the sea lanes and play an important role in the politics of the next twenty years. Launched when victory was in sight, she would represent the sunset glow of sea power—the last of the big ships whose presence on the horizon could determine policy. A lean silhouette reported off a coast line, she would be welcomed by the citizens of many countries and watched uneasily by those whose schemes were thwarted by her presence.

Ventis Secundis—With Favorable Winds—her ship's crest would read. Her name came from a family of great sailors. Most distinguished of them had been Viscount Samuel Hood, the Admiral whose actions against the French in the West Indies at the close of the eighteenth century were among the most brilliant of that, or almost any, war. Her name was also a tribute to Rear-Admiral the Honorable Horace Lambert Hood, third son of the fourth Viscount, and lineal descendant of the great Admiral. He had died at Jutland. A friend of Earl Beatty and leader of the Third Battle Cruiser Squadron, Rear-Admiral Hood had gone down aboard his ship the Invincible under the eyes of his

Commander-in-Chief. His widow, Lady Hood, launched the great ship.

No man living can avoid his fate, and ships too—which also have their characters and personalities—are subject to the same immutable laws. What strange operation of chance or fortune determined this ship's name? Here is an eyewitness account of the way in which Rear-Admiral Hood met his death in the Invincible.

> Hood pressed home his attack, and it was an inspiring sight to see this squadron of battle-cruisers dashing towards the enemy with every gun in action. On the Lion's bridge we felt like cheering them on, for it seemed that the decisive moment of the battle had come. Our feelings, however, suffered a sudden change, for just when success was in our grasp, the Invincible was hit by a salvo amidships. Several big explosions followed, great tongues of flame shot out from her riven side, the masts collapsed, the ship broke in two, and an enormous pall of black smoke rose to the sky. One moment she was the proud flagship full of life, intent on her prey; the next, she was just two sections of twisted metal, the bow and stern standing up out of the water like two large tombstones suddenly raised in honour of a thousand and twenty-six British dead; an astonishing sight, probably unique in naval warfare.*

It was not to be unique.

On that August launching day, with the gulls screaming over the disturbed water as the ship settled and the tugs took her, as the builders and the admirals and Admiral Hood's widow watched, and as the young apprentice kept his eyes on "his" plate on the starboard quarter, did no one feel a shiver down the spine? But then the launching of a great warship is always a moment of emotion. "A terrible beauty is born. . . ."

*Chalmers, *The Life and Letters of David, Earl Beatty*. Compare this description with the end of the Hood, page 193.

3

Her Ancestry

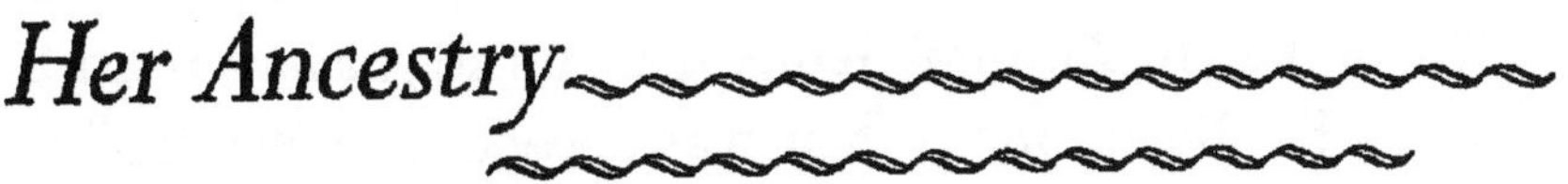

"There seems to be something wrong with our bloody ships today." With these words Admiral David Beatty turned to his flag captain Ernle Chatfield on the bridge of the battle cruiser Lion during the first part of the Battle of Jutland. What prompted them was the sight of the battle cruiser Queen Mary disappearing in a column of gray smoke while masts and funnels fell in over her broken back. "Like a toy in a pond," remarked one of the other eyewitnesses.

What were the lessons of Jutland? The question has often been asked, and the battle has been fought over on paper more than almost any other in British history. That fact in itself seems to prove that no one can consider Jutland a decisive victory. Little ink has been spilled over Trafalgar. Admiral Jellicoe may well have been the man who in Churchill's words could have "lost the war in an afternoon," but he was also the man who to a great extent could have won it.

The moment when Jellicoe's battle fleet turned away from the massed torpedo attack of the German destroyers was the moment when any possibility of an overwhelming victory was lost. In World War II it was accepted that in order to "comb the tracks" of torpedoes the best move was to turn toward them (thus presenting a narrow profile to attack). In this way the same limited profile was presented, but the range was shortened: the enemy was not allowed to make good an escape.

To be fair to Admiral Jellicoe, in turning away from the torpedoes, he did no more than was accepted as standard practice at the time by the Admiralty. The turn away was of course faulty tactical thinking, for it was a purely defensive measure, whereas the turn toward, being offensive, is clearly a better solution. In this respect alone Admiral Jellicoe must incur some of the responsibility for the unsatisfactory outcome of Jutland. The "turn-away" countermeasure against torpedo attack, which had been accepted by the Admiralty, was his own proposal.* The two other factors which emerge with clarity from an examination of the battle are the defective quality of British ammunition—not the gunnery itself—and the defective quality of the battle cruiser design.

On the gray day when the two greatest fleets in the world met in the unfriendly, muddy waters of the North Sea, the gunnery of the British fleet, and particularly of the battle cruisers, was of a high standard. As they knifed through the mist the lean ships under Beatty's command hit their opponents time and time again. The British sailors cheered as they saw—like fireworks bursting on a peaceful night—the orange glows flower and spread on the decks of their German opponents. Those sudden stars, had they but known it, were little to cheer about. They were shells failing to penetrate, shells that were doing little more than local damage or killing exposed personnel.

The successful shell in naval warfare is the one whose hit may never even be seen by the successful gunnery officer—which slices like a screaming drill through armor plate to explode inside a vessel and wound her mortally. It was with shells like these that the German High Seas Fleet hit the Grand Fleet. It

*Letter from Commander-in-Chief to Admiralty, October 30, 1914.

was a shell or a salvo with this deep piercing ability that took the lives of Admiral Hood and his men.

There was also "something wrong with our bloody ships," something that no amount of superior seamanship or morale (two qualities which the British had in full measure over their opponents) could counterbalance. The decks and turrets of the British battle cruisers were not sufficiently armored to withstand the plunging fire of modern armor-piercing shells.

In the past, naval actions had usually been fought at comparatively close ranges. In such circumstances it was essential that the sides of heavy ships should be well protected, for the flattish trajectory of the shells meant that their point of impact was likely to be the side of the opposing vessel. By the time that Jutland was fought, close-quarter engagements had become a thing of the past. The range at which most of the battle cruiser action was carried out was roughly seven and a half miles.* Shells striking the target at such a distance are inevitably plummeting or plunging on to their objective, and the armoring of the sides has become of less importance. It is the deck area which requires heavy protection. Furthermore, with the growth of the modern warship, the beam had considerably increased, thus making the deck area a much larger target than before. Defective design was the cause of the British losses in battle cruisers at Jutland. This is a point which can hardly be disputed, and it is one which Jellicoe made in his dispatch: "The facts which contributed to the British losses were, first, the indifferent armour protection of our battle-cruisers, particularly as regards turret armour and deck plating. . . ."

The ship that went down the ways on August 22, 1918, inherited the defects of her ancestry. It was over two years since the Battle of Jutland, but the lessons which the battle should

*In her last action against the Bismarck the Hood opened fire at nearly double this range—25,000 yards.

have taught had not been completely incorporated in her design. A few years later experts were to draw attention to the fact that the Hood suffered from some of the same defects which had accounted for the loss of the battle cruisers Indefatigable, Queen Mary, and Invincible. The solution was to increase the weight of her deck armor. For reasons which we will see, this was never done.

For over twenty years the "Mighty Hood"—as she was known to generations of sailors—suffered from a congenital weakness. The fault lay in her design—but she had been designed before Jutland. So for that matter had the German warships which took part in that action. In their case, though, Admiral von Tirpitz had stipulated that he would accept no design from his naval architects which was unable to pass a number of stringent and exhaustive tests. "Unsinkable gun platforms" was his requirement. This, as has been said, was easier for the Germans to accomplish than for the British. Nonetheless, the provision of adequate deck armor was equally possible for the British ships. It had little or no bearing on their inhabitability.

When the Hood was launched the future of the capital ship was very uncertain. Torpedoes, zeppelins, and aircraft now constituted a threat to sea power such as had never existed before. As long ago as 1918 there were many who maintained that the capital ship was doomed and that, in the future, warfare would be entirely determined by airborne missiles. It was not until the close of World War II that the death of the heavy ship was finally announced.

Historians prefer to record fact alone, maintaining that only recorded fact can be relied upon to give an indication of the history of man. Throughout her life, though, the Hood symbolized the greatness of her country, sea power, and might used benevolently. Those who are not professional historians may prefer to see in the history of her life and death not only the record of an inanimate creation of armored steel, but an expression of a world and of a way of life that has gone forever.

Even before she was first commissioned, the critics of heavy ships had filled their pens and—in the manner of retired military and naval men when the war is over—expressed those opinions which, until then, they had been compelled to keep to themselves. Ships like the Hood were under attack not only from ex-officers of the Royal Flying Corps and the Army, but even from Admirals of the Fleet.

May 1920, when the Hood was first commissioned, was no time for defenders of the capital ship to gain a fair hearing or—which was more important—to secure their point that more money should be allocated for them. As late as 1929 it was necessary for a defender of the battleship to adopt a forthright and pugilistic tone:

> It is a mistaken notion of an uninformed section of the Press and public that the battleship is a warship of a settled type and that, by reason of new forms of attack, this type is now, in great measure, obsolete. Actually the term "battleship" implies the "predominant surface ship," a warship which can hit harder, and better withstand all forms of attack than any other ship afloat. Logically, therefore, if the battleship is doomed any less powerful type of warship is doomed, because speed, the only quality in which lesser ships may be superior to the battleship, is obviously not an all-sufficient defense. If the battleship cannot keep the sea owing to the menace of the submarine or the aircraft, then neither can the cruiser, the destroyer, the aircraft carrier, nor patrol and escorting vessels. This can only lead to the conclusion that in a future war all surface vessels, especially unprotected merchant ships, are helpless, in which case the fate of the British Empire is already sealed. In reality this is very far from being the case, and the conception of the battleship as a senile leviathan retained by a conservative Admiralty is ridiculous. The battleship of today is the lineal descendant of the ship of the line of the sailing ship era, just as the cruiser is that of the frigate. Her

> business is to fight in company with ships of her own class, and the battle fleet is really the fulcrum on which the whole of sea power hinges; remove it, and the value of a surface fleet will be negligible in the face of an enemy with more powerful warships.*

World War II confirmed this viewpoint. In both the Mediterranean and the Pacific, the battleship's role was an important one and her function was far from being no more than a matter of containment of the enemy fleet. The invasions of Sicily, Anzio, and Salerno were facilitated by the bombardment power of capital ships. In the case of Salerno, the turning point of a fiercely opposed landing was largely due to the firepower of the fleet.

The Hood, then, throughout her nineteen years of peacetime life, was not a floating anachronism, but a potent weapon of war. She had the advantage over the nuclear rockets, now poised uneasily on their launching pads, in that she represented not only destruction, but also security for those who pass on the high seas "upon their lawful occasions."

The great advantage of the warship as a symbol of power was the fact that warships were manned by men—and men must eat, and drink, and go ashore, and meet other men. The role of the Hood during the interwar years was very much that of an ever-traveling ambassador. In this respect she was more successful than some of the constantly "on-the-wing" politicians and statesmen of recent years. The Foreign Secretary who arrives by air in another country lives only at V.I.P. level and meets only those of a similar caliber. The officers and men of a fleet or a great warship meet their foreign neighbors at every level from the dockyard tavern to the sports ground and the Ambassador's residence. The success of "showing the flag" cruises can be

*William J. Berry in the *Encyclopaedia Britannica,* 14th edition (1929), when Director of Naval Construction, Admiralty, 1929; also Director of Warship Production, 1917-23. Reprinted by permission of the publishers.

judged by one fact alone, that our relationships with South American countries have never been so friendly, nor so easy, since they came to an end.

Even more terribly than the Hood, the hidden rocket and the supersonic H-bomber represent power. We live under their shadow, but the disastrous fact is that there is less contact than ever before between the men who wield these weapons of war and the people of their own, let alone of other, countries. The Hood, cleaving the bright waters off Montevideo, may have been awe-inspiring, but she was beautiful. The men who came ashore were soon found to be similar to other men anywhere, with the same weaknesses and the same strengths. Although they moved the greatest warship in the world, they were also men who desired only to live in peace and in friendship with their neighbors. Year in, year out, over the oceans and in the seaports of the world the ship's company of the Hood proved that power can be benevolent. Such an achievement is rare.

It was in May 1941 that she sailed on her last voyage. It is another one of the curious signs of her fated history that it was also in May, exactly twenty-one years before, that she had set out on her first. On each occasion she went north, and on each occasion her port of departure was Scapa Flow.

The Flow was still being used as a fleet training ground and base in 1920, and the Hood as she stood out to sea—a new ship working up to her full efficiency—was to carry many lives in her hull, and influence many men, before she sailed again from those same islands for the last time. The rocks and inlets and cropped grass of the Orkneys are still the same under the spring sun as they were in 1941—or in 1920.

> Only thin smoke without flame
> From the heaps of couch grass;
> Yet this will go onward the same
> Though Dynasties pass.

On June 21, 1919, the main units of the German High Seas Fleet, which had been interned in Scapa Flow, were scuttled and abandoned by their crews. The rust was still bright on their superstructures, which jutted from the water, when the new ship got under way. Passing the ruins of a fleet, she headed for the North Sea.

Flying the flag of Acting Vice-Admiral Sir Roger Keyes, the new battle cruiser left on the first of her many courtesy visits. She was accompanied by the Tiger, a battle cruiser that had joined Admiral Beatty's flag in 1914. The two capital ships were flanked by an escort of nine destroyers. They were bound from the old Norse islands of the Orkneys for the birthplace of all long ships, Scandinavia. From Nynäshamn, twenty-five miles from Stockholm, they would proceed to Copenhagen and thence to Norway. The kings of those countries would be there to meet them.

4

Mediterranean Cruise

In 1955 I was sitting in the London Bar looking out along Main Street, Gibraltar, with the people coming and going, and a pale sunlight gleaming on the wet road. Over by Algeciras the land was hard and gold and bright, but here the levanter cloud was only just lifting and the light was fitful, like an English June.

"I remember," said old Gomez, "what it was like when we hear that time that the Hood is sunk." He pointed at the photograph of her hanging behind the bar. "I am living in the Fulham Road, London. My wife and I are evacuated because we are too old to stay on the Rock during the war. We hear it over the B.B.C. when we are sitting in a pub. . . . I think the world has come to an end! I truly think that we are finished, señor. If the Germans can sink *her,* then there is no more hope, I say to myself. And yet—here I am back in my old bar again!"

"You remember the Hood?"

"Of course! Often here before the war. I remember the first time I see her and she is the biggest ship I ever see. I'm working for the laundry in those days and we go aboard to collect the officers' things. I remember how big she is and how the decks so clean you could eat off them. Clean like a polished window!"

He drew off a glass of sherry for himself. "Long time ago those days, 'Nother world, eh? You don' remember, too young?"

"Eighteen when the war broke out."

"Same age as me first time I go aboard the Hood. Everything's different then. Tell you how—not only the ships is bigger, there's more 'bull,' you know? More brass work, eh, more men scrubbing decks, officers very gentlemanly—they don't do too much, eh? Now'days officers much the same as the men, not then. And when the ship's com'ny comes ashore they drink more than now, but more discipline if they go back drunk. Today they comes here and they are not sailors like they was—mostly quiet young men. I get some even tells me what type of sherry they likes. Not in them days, señor. If they drinks sherry then—just like beer. Half-pint glass!

"Great boxers in the Hood," he said, coming back from serving another customer. "She had more men than the other ships, that's true, but the Hood was always winning the fleet championships. All changed now. Sailors is different."

"Nowadays it's radar and rockets," I said. "You don't find the old type any more."

"Different the days when I'm talking about—when I used to go over for the laundry. Another world."

The Hood was always a great boxing ship, good at all sports come to that, but she had early made a reputation for producing some of the best boxers in the fleet. In September 1922, when she was visiting Rio de Janeiro, the British boxing contingent beat the United States by four bouts to three. Five of the fighters came from the Hood, and three of them won their matches.

In the early spring of 1921 the same dull plume of a levanter cloud hung over the Rock of Gibraltar. Down below, in the narrow streets, the gray drizzle leeched along the brick fronts and dampened the bar signs and the shops in Main Street. "The English," as the Spaniards say, "take their own weather with them."

The great ships were standing into harbor—the battle cruisers

Hood and Tiger, with their jinking, keen-bowed escort of destroyers taking the spray over their fo'c's'les as they moved into position. The battle cruiser squadron had come south for a Mediterranean cruise.

In those days no crackling voice over the ship's loud-speaker system roused the sailors from their hammocks in the morning. It was the birdlike trill of the bosun's call, or the brass voice of the bugle, that cut through their sleep. Lying at anchor, with her decks steaming gently as the night dew lifted, a ship like the Hood came to life with an efficiency that required the planning and organizing ability of many brains. Before the hands had fallen in at their parts of the ship, for cleaning and shining their steel home, the cooks in the galleys were already busy preparing breakfast. With a plock and gurgle, steam heat was being turned on in vast caldrons to boil water for tea.

"Tanky and his men," the supply department's working parties, were busy rigging tackles and hoisting from holds and refrigerators the sugar, flour, carcasses of meat, and other supplies that would be required throughout the day. Aft in the admiral's quarters, his senior steward was laying the tray with the admiral's early morning tea. "This one," he had to remember, "likes wafer-thin brown bread and butter with it." (The last had liked China tea with lemon and two biscuits.)

The tampions—those brass symbols of peace that fitted over the dark mouths of the 15-inch guns and bore the ship's crest—were being polished. The hoses were splashing along the decks, while sailors with their bell bottoms rolled up were scrubbing down under the eyes of petty officers.

"You get any water on that bright work, and you're in the rattle, Jackson!"

"Aye, aye, Chief! (Got a thick 'ead this morning, ain't 'e?)"

"You're in the rattle if you talks instead of works—and don't forget it!"

It was early spring and the ship's company were still in their blue uniforms. The officer of the morning watch was seeing that the logbook had been filled in correctly by the gangway staff: the barometer reading, the wet and dry air temperatures, and the note, "0600. Hands called." There was a dispatch boat coming out from the long arm of the breakwater and he put his telescope on it, the brass rim striking fire out of the morning sunlight. Beyond the breakwater the bald limestone head of the Rock lifted against a lilac sky. The levanter that had been blowing when the ships came in the day before had died away. The wind had veered round to the south, hot off Africa across the Strait.

Captured by British and Dutch forces in 1704, during the War of the Spanish Succession, Gibraltar had dominated the Strait for more than two hundred years—and in a way that it can never do again. This craggy outcrop at the foot of Spain, along with the point of Ceuta on the African coast, had been famed since classical times, when the two giant rocks guarding the entrance to the Mediterranean had been known as the Pillars of Hercules. Beyond them began that terrifying world of vast seas, of strange water movements that ebbed and flowed with the moon—the incomprehensible surge of tides and tidal races that was to bewilder the Romans in their later campaigns. Beyond the Pillars of Hercules even the Phoenicians, those master mariners of the ancient world, were never able to feel at home.

Out of the distant northern island, once the farthest dependency of the Roman Empire, had come these gray steel ships to patrol and dominate the tideless Mediterranean Sea. It was in May 1921, only a few weeks after Hood's visit to Gibraltar, that Benito Mussolini and thirty-five other Fascist candidates were returned at the Italian elections. It is hardly surprising that these leaders of a movement designed to restore Italy's greatness regarded a ship like the Hood as a symbol of her present inferiority. The presence of foreign warships in the sea that had once belonged to Rome was naturally resented by the Fascist party. Some years were to pass before they would make the bold claim that the Mediterranean was *Mare Nostrum.* By then the shipbuilding yards of Genoa and the aircraft factories of Milan would have produced the power to reinforce this claim.

After leaving Gibraltar that year the Hood went on to Málaga, Valencia, and Toulon. A report on the cruise says: "Many guests were entertained on board the ships at the various ports, and the ships' companies were well received on the shore by the local inhabitants." Like most official reports it tells us little about the real life of the ship during those months. It is curious to think, looking at logbooks and diaries kept during this period, that this was the heyday of the Roaring Twenties. Little of it is reflected in naval records, and the social historian who had nothing else to rely on would carry away a curious and unbalanced picture of the times. Much more than the Army—which, after all, must live ashore even if it still lives in its own withdrawn community—the Navy had a specialized existence, remote from the preoccupations of the land.

This was the era described by the young Evelyn Waugh, by Noel Coward, Michael Arlen, F. Scott Fitzgerald, and Ernest Hemingway—the wasteland of frustrated hopes, emasculated heroes, sun-tanned nymphomaniacs, and bottle-scarred veterans. Little of it seems to have made its imprint on the self-contained community of a great warship, under the shadow of whose presence, far out at sea, the uneasy peace of those lotus-eating years was maintained.

Like a cocktail made with too much Italian vermouth, Michael Arlen's *Green Hat* preserves something of the flavor of the era, and portrays a naval officer of the period: "His eyes slightly bloodshot, not so much from hours of scanning distant horizons, as from too many pink gins in the wardroom—there being so little else to do in battleships."

There was, of course, plenty to do, but the round of entertaining from one port to another caused many officers to sigh at the prospect of yet another "good-will" cruise. "Entertaining and being entertained is all very well," wrote Admiral Cunningham in his autobiography.* "but a few days of high-pressure official engagements and entertainments from 9:30 A.M. one morning until 3 or 4 A.M. the next makes the average naval man long to get away to sea. Courtesy visits to foreign ports and 'Showing the Flag' cruises do a great deal of good; but they are among the most strenuous exercises I know, and ruinous to the digestion."

From Gibraltar to Málaga is 62 miles. As they swept up the coast on a day of bright sunlight, with their escorting destroyers on their flanks, the two British battle cruisers made a fine sight. The V-headed arrows of their wakes interleaved and crisscrossed astern of them. Inshore, where the open rowing boats of the coastal fishermen lingered with lines down over the shallow banks, the thunder of the long swell came in to break on the rocks as if, far out to sea, a gale were blowing.

On trials the Hood had achieved a speed of 31.9 knots at deep-load draft, and 32.07 at local draft. She was always a fast ship—that was what she had been designed to be—but she was also remarkable for another factor, her high economical speed. This was something that endeared her to engineer officers, especially during the stringencies of those postwar days, when every official return was scrutinized to see whether there had been any waste. At only two-fifths power the Hood could steam at 25 knots—those other three fifths were all needed to drive her 44,000 tons just 6 or 7 knots faster. The power: fuel ratio, in large ships especially, often gives a surprising graph: the extra fuel, power, and space to accommodate them are all required to provide those last few knots. At 25 knots, though, the Hood was happy, and so was the engineer captain. So too were the officers and crew, for she had surprisingly little vibration at her economical cruising speed.

*Cunningham, *A Sailor's Odyssey*.

It was the sacrifices in her armor to give her those additional knots that distressed a writer to the *Naval Review:**

> In the case of the Hood the whole of the increased displacement has been allocated to one factor—speed. A change of policy is thus established, and it is one whose nature the writer holds to be unjustified by either tactical or strategical considerations.

If the Hood's design had been agreed upon at the time when this writer voiced his criticism (1920), then he would have been right in condemning what he calls a "change of policy." His error was to have forgotten that the Hood was laid down in 1916, before the lessons of Jutland had been fully appreciated, and that she did not represent a change of policy but the continuation of an earlier one.

Later, in this same analysis of the value of speed in capital ships, the writer makes the point that

> We are told by her designer that experience and trial have shown that the Hood can receive the blows of several torpedoes and still remain in the line without serious loss of speed.

If one examines her lines, her protective bulges, and her underwater armor plating, this would seem to have been true.

As she dropped anchor under the tawny lion-skin walls of Gibralfaro castle, in Málaga, power was what she represented to the Spaniards watching, and to the Spanish admiral whose barge went out to meet her. But power, as the writer in the *Naval Review* had remarked, must be looked at in two ways.

> Power to withstand punishment is alike necessary to the pugilist and the capital ship. Speed must never be permitted to develop at the expense of protection.

In that first Mediterranean cruise, the foreign naval officers and the distinguished visitors, as well as the general public, found much to marvel at in this graceful giant. For the gunnery

*"Value of Speed in Capital Ships," *Naval Review,* Vol. 8, No. 2 (1920).

specialist there were the eight 15-inch guns in their huge turrets, guns whose shells weighed a ton apiece and whose muzzle velocity was 1,670 miles per hour. For the engineer the gleaming engine rooms demanded inspection; the brass voice pipes gleaming, the ladder rungs shining silver, and the polished dials and indicators that returned your reflection on every hand. Boiler rooms murmured that the whitewashed lagging on pipes was not for greasy hands, and auxiliary machinery thrummed. Beyond were housed her four turbine engines—four turbines developing a total of 144,000 h.p., each unit driving its 20-ton propeller.

For those with a taste for astronomical figures there were her six vast searchlights, each of 120,000,000 candle power, designed for the kind of night action that would never be seen again. By the time World War II started, British scientists and technicians would have evolved radio direction finding, or radar; the night and the fog would be pierced without a ray of light.

The cap tallies bearing the words "H.M.S. Hood" became familiar in the streets and on the waterfronts of the Mediterranean. At Toulon, which was the northernmost point of that spring cruise, the French *matelots* thought, perhaps, that there were far too many of them in the town. (Today it is the American fleet that they complain about.)

It was in the August of this year 1921, shortly after the Hood's cruise had finished, that Sir Eric Geddes was appointed chairman of a committee which was to affect the lives of many of the officers and men then serving aboard her. A businessman whom Lloyd George had enlisted under his banner in 1915, Geddes was an able administrator and an efficient organizer. He had streamlined British communication and supply lines in France during the war and, as Controller of the Admiralty in the spring of 1917, he had co-ordinated and centralized the shipbuilding resources of the country—much as Lord Beaverbrook was to do for aircraft production during World War II. Subsequently Geddes had been First Lord of the Admiralty for a short time, and then

President of the newly formed Ministry of Transport. This was the man whose name would be immortalized as the wielder of the "Geddes Ax," that system of economies in public expenditure from which the Navy, more than almost any other service, was to suffer.

When the Hood completed her first Mediterranean cruise the harsh edge of the Geddes Ax was still concealed. So was the Washington Treaty. After them, nothing would ever be quite the same again. The decks might still shine white under the sun, the gunnery control be more efficient, the communications system be improved—a hundred and one other things. But, Great Britain would no longer be the first naval power.

5

Politicians and Others

In July 1921 President Harding invited Great Britain, France, Italy, and Japan to a conference at Washington on the limitation of national armaments. Secretary of State Hughes, Elihu Root, and Senators Lodge and Underwood represented the United States. Mr. Balfour (as he then was), together with Lord Lee of Fareham, Sir Auckland Geddes, and Sir Robert Borden, represented Great Britain. The importance of the Washington Conference to this history is that if the Hood during her long life represented in many ways the last sunset glow of the *Pax Britannica* throughout the world, this conference was one of the many signs that that long-lasting supremacy upon the seas no longer obtained. The reasons why Britain had for so long been able to maintain this peace (until shattered by World War I) have been succinctly put by F. H. Hinsley:*

> It was the combined power of geography, fleets, and finance which enabled her statesmen to wield for so long an influence which approached, if it did not quite attain, the dimensions of world sovereignty and world order.

We shall see nothing like it again until such a time as a world state may be established.

*Hinsley, *Command of the Sea.*

The conference opened on November 12, 1921. The American Secretary of State immediately proposed that "for a period of not less than ten years there shall be no further construction of capital ships." Admirals Beatty and Chatfield, who were representing Britain's naval interests at the conference, were not so much concerned about capital ships as about the potential limitation of cruisers. On cruisers, more than anything else, the life lines of the Empire depended. Britain accepted the limitation on capital ships, therefore, with the proviso that the quality of her ships should not be allowed to fall behind that of other nations.

At this period the capital ship was fiercely criticized, many maintaining that its day was over and done with. This school of thought completely overlooked the fact that the capital ship was no more than the largest unit of a fleet, and that so long as other countries possessed them a country like Britain, dependent on its overseas communications, must have them as well. In World War II the activities of German pocket battleships, or full-sized battleships, would have gone completely unhampered if the Admiralty had succumbed to the idea that the capital ship was obsolete. As it was, we entered the war gravely handicapped with respect to capital ships, and with a high proportion of those which we possessed almost obsolete, or certainly obsolescent.

On December 20 agreement was reached between the contracting parties that the United States and Great Britain should maintain naval parity with 525,000 tons of capital ships each; Japan should have 315,000 tons, and Italy and France 175,000 tons each. The Japanese had fought hard to secure their additional tonnage, which was accepted only on the condition that Britain should be allowed to build two new vessels (of not more than 35,000 tons each) while the United States should complete two ships already in process of construction. The two new ships built by Britain were the famous Nelson and Rodney, sometimes known as the "Washington ships" because their truncated appearance was dictated by the tonnage limitations imposed by the treaty. The Washington Treaty was thus indirectly responsible for the fact that the Hood, with her 42,000 tons, remained throughout her life the largest capital ship afloat.

Mr. Balfour proposed the complete abolition of submarines. It was very natural that he should, seeing that the submarine had already proved itself the greatest menace to England's security. It is part of the whole curiously unreal world of the Washington Conference, however, that he should have bothered to make the proposal. Was it likely that any potential aggressor against Britain or the Empire was going to accept even a limitation on submarine building? We forget, perhaps, the balmy climate of those days, when the soft airs and zephyrs blowing from Geneva had induced the belief—even among hardheaded statesmen and politicians—that we were all on the brink of a new world order. War was to be outlawed, peace and right thinking would prevail. The Americans, with their somewhat Rousseauesque concept of the innate nobility of man, have always been predisposed to this type of optimism. In those immediate postwar years they were absorbed in their dream world of the "big rock candy mountains."

If they were prepared to agree with Britain on the subject of no limitation on the number of cruisers which might be built, it was only on the condition that the maximum limit should be 10,000 tons with 8-inch guns. From the British point of view this was most unsatisfactory. A greater number of cruisers, of lesser tonnage and more lightly armed, would have served our purpose better.

Optimism reigned in those days, and the atmosphere of Washington was heady with it. This is borne out by such clauses in the treaty as Number 17:

> In the event of a Contracting Power being engaged in war, such Power shall not use as a vessel of war any vessel of war which may be under construction within its jurisdiction for any other Power, or which may have been constructed within its jurisdiction for another Power.

Was it conceivable that, in the event of war, any country would have paid attention to such a clause? It might have been better if the treaty discussions had taken place in a more realistic capital, such as London.

Not that London was noticeably clearheaded at the time. Admiral Beatty, aware that behind his back politicians and journalists were supporting the campaign for Britain to give the world a lead in the reduction of armaments, returned to England to lend the weight of his authority to the opposite party. Admiral Chatfield remained behind at Washington to deal with the remaining items on the agenda. Britain owes a great deal to these two Admirals for their clear thinking and hardheadedness during a difficult time.

It was not only the conclusions reached about cruiser building which were a blow to Britain; the most important and far-reaching consequence of the Washington Treaty was the termination of the Anglo-Japanese Alliance. This alliance had been signed in 1902, and had been designed to contain Russian ambitions in the Far East. Imperial Russia had always pursued the same aims that have subsequently been adopted by Soviet Russia; her interests not being confined to Europe and the Balkans but, then as now, to China, Korea, Japan, and the Pacific. The treaty had provided for mutual assistance in safeguarding British and Japanese interests in China and Korea. It had proved invaluable to Japan during the Russo-Japanese war of 1904, and it had been revised to cover India and Eastern Asia generally a year later. The treaty had resulted in Japan's immediate entrance into World War I on the Allied side. It had produced other noteworthy results, particularly in terms of Anglo-Japanese friendship, which had made for stabilizing conditions in the Pacific and the Far East. The treaty, as might be expected, was extremely unpopular in China. It was almost equally unpopular in the United States.

One of the factors which must be faced in any history of the twentieth century is that the decline of Britain as a world power owes its origins not only to two disastrous wars, but also to economic and trade rivalry with America. Many Americans disliked the Anglo-Japanese Treaty because they already saw the Pacific as a sphere of American influence. Their business and commercial organizations disliked the predominance of British goods—as well as British ships—in the Far East. Therefore, at the Washington Conference, the strongest pressure was brought upon Britain to abrogate the Anglo-Japanese Treaty, replacing it by a Four Power Pacific Treaty (the United States, the British Empire, France, and Japan). In December 1921 this Four Power Agreement was ratified and the Anglo-Japanese Alliance terminated.

There were many in Britain, of course, who saw the new treaty as thoroughly satisfactory, reducing—as it did—our commitments in the Far East and thus enabling us to carry on with the economies in our services that had been initiated by Sir Eric Geddes. These were the years when a large section of the press and the public saw every Army officer as a "Colonel Blimp," and every admiral as a ludicrous kind of "Grogram"—both of them equally bent on preserving an absurd old-fashioned institution known as the British Empire. The termination of the Anglo-Japanese Alliance was hardly noticed in the British press at the time. It led ultimately to that American-Japanese rivalry in the Pacific which contributed in no small measure to World War II. The movement of one small stone on a mountain may not be remarked by the villagers living below, but it may sometimes cause a landslide.

There were other disastrous consequences of the Washington Treaty, and none which afflicted the Royal Navy more than the so-called "Ten-Year Rule." This was a formula for governments, based on the assumption that there would be no major war for at least ten years. It was annually renewed from 1923 until 1932—by which time the evidence of world events had become clear.

The rule provided a basis for service estimates, and was undoubtedly the major cause for the decline of our fighting power during these years. It weakened the Navy, influenced foreign policy, and was finally to lead, at the London Naval Conference of 1930, to the major stupidity of those interwar years—when Britain agreed to reduce her cruiser strength to parity with the United States. In 1930 the efforts that Admirals Beatty and Chatfield had made to insure that our life lines were not weakened were finally nullified.

The climate of opinion fostered by the Washington Treaty, the Ten-Year Rule, and the conference of 1930 was such that all ships in commission may be said to have suffered equally. By the 1930's, it had become clear that the Hood needed a major refit to bring her into line with modern conditions of warfare. It was known that her deck armor needed substantial reinforcing, and that her secondary armament and her control system needed bringing up to date. By the thirties, however, it was too late. As one crisis succeeded another throughout the world it became unthinkable that the "Mighty Hood" should be put out of commission for a long time.

The Hood's life must be seen against the background of her times. Politics and conferences may seem remote from the lives of her officers and men, yet in fact they were not. Just as political considerations determined her movements throughout the years, so they determined her strength and her fitness. The Washington Treaty insured that the Hood remained the greatest ship afloat, the most powerful unit in the world—but it was a world whose balance had almost imperceptibly shifted.

6

The Sea Life

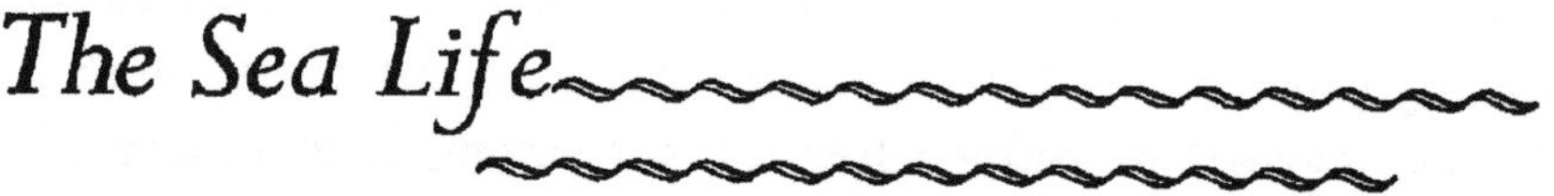

"When men come to like a sea life they are not fit to live on land," remarked Dr. Johnson, but then the Doctor was, for an Englishman, curiously averse to the sea. The "sea life" of a great warship like the Hood was indeed a far remove from life ashore. Although there are still great ships like aircraft carriers afloat, it is strange to think that, less than a quarter of a century later, the type of life lived by the sailors aboard the Hood already seems remote. Even by 1939 the sailor's life was fast changing, and in recent years many of the old ways and traditions have gone forever.

In peacetime the average establishment for the Hood was some 70 officers, 480 seamen, 60 boys, 180 marines, 300 engine-room ratings, and 60 to 70 nonexecutive ratings (which included supply branch assistants, sick berth attendants, etc.). The officers had their wardroom below the main searchlight platform, forward of the captain's and the admiral's quarters. They were served from their own separate galley and pantry, as were the warrant officers in their mess and the midshipmen in the gunroom. The catering for the officers' messes was usually left in the hands of a petty officer steward, known as the messman. He was responsible for all the special buying and provisioning, as well as organizing the basic rations. (Lowerdeck legend had it that all messmen salted enough away to buy themselves a quiet pub ashore to which one day they would retire!)

Chief and petty officers had their own messes, Spartan in their simplicity, but allowing each man some room for his private effects and gear. The bulk of the ship's company lived in large open spaces, known as broadside messes, with a leading seaman responsible for each mess and presiding over each table. The tables themselves were scrubbed white every day and could be detached from the deck and secured by lashings to the deckhead if need be. Like the chief and petty officers, the sailors slept in hammocks, but this was no hardship. When the ship was in a seaway the man in his hammock slept safe and sound while the officer with his "comfortable bunk" was forced to wedge himself in with pillows and clothing.

The sailor's hammock contains a mattress with a mattress cover and is lashed up every day before the hands fall in, and stowed in a hammock netting. At night after "pipe down," when all the hammocks are slung in a messdeck, a visitor must make his way, stooping, under the dark bundles that sway from the hammock hooks over his head. When it is cold the hammock makes a snug bed, its canvas sides closing up round the sleeper and keeping him in a warm nest. In hot weather some of the sailors prefer to lay their hammocks out on the deck, but the majority keep themselves cool by putting a wooden "spreader" bar between the "nettles" or lashings at each end of the hammock, so that it is kept open and presents a flatter surface. Each sailor has two of these canvas hammocks which must be changed and scrubbed regularly, and the hammock lashing and the "nettles" at head and foot must also be kept scrupulously clean.

As always where there are old-time sailors, devices or "tiddley" work have been invented to improve a standard issue. No long-service able seaman worth his salt would have a hammock lashing that was not beautifully pointed and grafted, so that it became more than a simple rope but a minor work of art.

Throughout the ship, wherever there was the opportunity for such rope work, a leading seaman or an old A.B. would make it a matter of pride to show the "youngsters" how it was done. The tiller handles of the boats were enlivened by fancy rope work, Turk's-heads, and diamond patterns; the heads of gangways were also ornamented; so too were boat hooks, fenders, and fender lanyards.

The natural instinct of man is to adorn his surroundings, and the sailor was adept at it at a time when most of his relatives ashore in an urban society were forgetting the exercises of the crafts that had once made the villages of England beautiful. The hammock itself was a legacy from the West Indies, and had been adopted by British warships in the eighteenth century, after their sailors had found the native Caribs taking their ease in hammocks slung between the trees.

Another Carib contribution to civilization which played an important part in a sailor's life was tobacco. Although an able seaman's pay during these years was only 3*s.* a day, he was issued every month with tobacco at only 1*s.* 10*d.* a pound. This, along with his rum, was one of the sailor's chief privileges, and even in those days, when the duty was less than now, was not inconsiderable. Tobacco was issued in two forms, in tins made up either as a pipe or cigarette mixture, or in leaf. The half-pound tins of tobacco were known as "Tickler's," after a famous Grimsby firm which had supplied the Navy during the 1914–18 war with jam in somewhat similar tins. Leaf tobacco was made up into "pricks," a strong black plug which the old-timers preferred to the lighter mixture in "Tickler's." Making up a "prick" of tobacco was an art in itself, one that was dying out by 1939 and is now completely extinct, leaf tobacco no longer being issued. First the leaves were carefully trimmed and then laid into a hammock-shaped strip of canvas. Some sailors saved a little of their rum issue to dampen the leaves and give them a flavor, while others swore that the spirit in the rum ruined the tobacco. The whole parcel was then lashed up as tightly as possible and left for some weeks, or even months, for the leaves to mature and form a solid block.

"Grog," as every landman knows, is the sailor's rum issue, called after the nickname of Admiral Vernon, who first decreed that the issue should be diluted with water. The idea behind this dilution was to prevent sailors storing up their rum and then going on a bender—the admixture of water with the rum insuring that it would not keep in the same way as the pure spirit. Chief and petty officers alone were allowed the privilege of drawing "neaters" (neat rum), three parts water to one of spirit being the issue for all other ratings. On the occasion of a birthday, or if some sailor had had an addition to his family, or, perhaps, done some unwelcome chore for another, the cry would go up that he wanted "sippers." Strictly illegal, since each sailor is supposed to drink his rum in front of the issuing officer (which was not always possible), "sippers" meant that he was entitled to sip from the mug of his messmate.

At this time the Navy was in the process of changing to what was known as "General Messing," a system whereby the paymaster and his staff were responsible for the planning of all the ship's meals. The old method had been for each cook of the mess to prepare individual meals for his messmates, taking them to the galley to be cooked. In ships the size of the Hood such a system obviously made for wastage and confusion, and the General Messing system was gradually adopted throughout the fleet. The sailor had his own name for favorite dishes—"duff" was always steamed pudding, a dish which sailors could down with the greatest apparent ease even in tropical conditions. "Tiddey-oggey" was a Cornish pasty, and as such favored by Devonport ratings (who were reputed to be weaned on it). "Pot mess" was any kind of stew. This led to the term becoming part of the sailor's slang, and being applied to any situation or muddle where it was difficult to see what was going on; for instance, if the ship had come alongside a quay inefficiently it would be said: "The Old Man got himself in a regular 'pot mess' this morning." "Nutty," a term originally applied to the bars of nut chocolate in which the N.A.A.F.I. canteen specialized, finally came to cover the whole range of chocolates and sweets. "Ky" was always cocoa, a favorite drink of sailors, especially on cold nights, and made in the Navy from heavy slab chocolate flaked down with a knife and added to a mixture of condensed milk, sugar, and boiling water. The finest "ky" makers maintained that, if it was properly made, a spoon placed vertical in the center of the cup would hesitate for a moment before falling slowly and gently to the side. "Goffers" was the sailor's generic term for all soft drinks. In hot weather when the N.A.A.F.I. would open a side hatch for the supply of orange, lime, and lemon drinks, this section became known as the "goffer bar." Because of its association with something soft and nonalcoholic, the expression "He's only good for goffers!" became a term of abuse.

Sailors' language, as was natural among a specialized race of men, contained innumerable slang terms and words, so much so that conversation on the lowerdeck would have been almost incomprehensible to an outsider. "The jaunty," or "johnty," was the master-at-arms, a much maligned chief petty officer who was in charge of the ship's regulating staff and, consequently, responsible for its discipline. "The jaunty" was always present at the reading out of all warrants, whenever a sailor was sentenced to detention or other disciplinary measures. The petty officers who worked on the regulating staff were known as "crushers," the name supposedly dating back to the old days when naval ships were full of cockroaches. It was said that the stealthy tread of the regulating staff checking the ship for misdemeanors could be detected by the regular crunch-crunch-crunch of their "beetle crushers" (feet) on the cockroach-paved decks.

"My party" was the sailor's name for his regular girl or fiancée, and "my oppo" for his "opposite number" or close friend.

"Towney," an expression of regard, was accorded to those who came from the same town or village. Inhabitants of Liverpool were always known as "Scouse,"* all Welshmen as "Taff," Scots as "Jock," and Irish as "Paddy." Individual names also had their relevant "tallies"—Clarke being "Nobby," White "Shiner," Green "Jimmy," Adams "Fanny," and so on. The three remaining establishments from which ratings were drawn also had their nicknames: "Chatty" for (Dirty) Chatham, "Pompey" for Portsmouth, and "Guz" for Devonport.

In charge of each mess was a leading seaman, known as a "killick" (little anchor) from the badge on his arm. He was responsible for seeing that the men under him kept their mess clean and tidy. As well as checking the neat stowage of the hammocks, he had to see that all the kitchen gear and implements allocated to them were spotlessly clean and sufficient in numbers. There was an enameled container for the bread, a large teapot, and a shipside locker for tea, sugar, and cocoa. There were also a number of oval or round mess tins known as "fannies" used for collecting and serving the food. These had to be shined and burnished to equal the bright work of the ship itself.

The sailor had little space for his own belongings. In a ship like the Hood he had a locker and a small, scrubbed whitewood box known as a "ditty box," in which he kept letters, photographs, writing equipment, and other private possessions. The box bore a polished brass label with the sailor's name on the lid, and inside almost invariably were pinned pictures of his wife and children.

Tattooing was still popular, and some of the old hands could boast of tattoos from almost every port in the world—an eagle on the chest from Hong Kong, a girl's name from Sydney, a foul anchor on the right wrist from Portsmouth, a tombstone even, with the recorded dates of some loved one, on the forearm. Elab-

*From lobscouse, a kind of hash served aboard sailing ships in the nineteenth century.

orate tattoos were an object of pride to many old-timers. I remember one long-service leading seaman who bore across his back the scene of a fox hunt, stretching from the top of his right shoulder blade, the fox going to earth lower down.

Within a few weeks of the ship commissioning, small communities of specialist tradesmen soon established themselves. Firms who undertook tailoring jobs and made new suits were common, so too were "snobs" or cobblers. Sailors took great pride in their uniform, still the most dashing of any of the services, and would spend several pounds on "shore-going" suits, smarter and better cut than the standard issue from the "pusser's" (paymaster's) store.

The sailor's best suit was known as his Number One's, and the really "tiddley" sailor was never content with the Admiralty regulation cut. Technically the bell-bottom trousers were supposed to be 28 inches round the trouser bottoms, but the smart "Jack Ashore" preferred 32 inches or even 34 inches which gave his trousers more of a swing and roll when promenading. Sometimes zealous officers, inspecting the men before shore leave, would try to insure that only regulation trousers were being worn. With the regulation 28-inch bell bottom, the toecap of the shoe was still visible, but the 32-inch bottom covered it completely. Standing at attention then, the "tiddley" sailor, to escape detection, would pull back the overflow of his trousers between his knees and keep it held there until the inspection was over. He would hope that the inspecting officer, seeing enough regulation toecap, would not notice that the trousers were oversize. A refinement practiced only by the most dandified was to sew small pieces of lead or halfpennies at the edges of the trouser bottoms. This increased their swagger when walking out.

The regulation blue jumper was also considered by the smart to have too high a neckline and not show a deep enough breadth of chest. This could be remedied by making the V of the jumper a good deal deeper. Again, an inspection could be passed by the simple expedient of fitting "poppers," or a hook and eye, a little higher up, so that the V appeared to be no deeper than normal. Once off the ship, and the jumper was adjusted.

The sailor's black "silk" had to be immaculately ironed, the white lanyard pristine, and there was an art to the tying of the butterfly cap bow. A perfectly shaped bow may have taken as long as an hour to cut and tie. Under his jumper the sailor wore the regulation white flannel with its dark blue piping round the neck. Although it was illegal, some of the "tiddleys" would wear dickey fronts (rather like a waiter's) which were secured by tapes round the chest, and were cooler in hot weather. The cap had to be worn straight on between the eyes and slightly down-tilted toward the nose, but once ashore those with panache would quickly give it an edge to one side or the other, or set it back on the head with a quiff of hair protruding in front. On the best suits all badges and good-conduct stripes were in gold braid; red-tape badges were for the ordinary working suit.

Such a world was a narrow one, but it produced men of fine character and loyalties. Loyalty to the ship was a driving force above all others, and a happy ship was every sailor's dream. In her long life Hood had her ups and downs, but in the main she always seems to have been remembered by those who served aboard her as a happy ship. The officers in charge of each division, and the chief and petty officers who worked under them, were largely responsible for such a state of affairs. The executive ratings or upperdeck sailors were assigned on arrival to one of three divisions— fo'c's'le, top, and quarterdeck—which took their names from the old parts of ship in the days of sail.

The backbone of the ship were undoubtedly the long-service ratings and especially the chief and petty officers. In those days a large percentage of the men had joined as boys, and knew more on leaving their boys' training than many an able seaman today. From the age of eighteen, men signed on for twelve years' service;

hence "Roll on my twelve" became the expression which greeted all disagreeable chores. After "the twelve" was up, a man could sign on for an additional ten years, at the end of which he was entitled to draw a pension. Seamen in their second period of service, and there were many of them in the Hood during these years, were trained and experienced men with a finger-tip knowledge of their profession. The old expression applied to dyed-in-the-wool sailors, "Every finger a marlinspike and every hair a bunch of spunyarn," could really be applied to such men. They were a living tradition, and without them the incredible expansion of the Navy during the last war could never have taken place.

I remember a typical figure, "Shiner" White, who was a three-badge able seaman aboard the Harrow in 1941. In a ship's company composed almost entirely of "H.O.'s"—Hostilities Only ratings—Shiner was worth six ordinary men. He taught their trade to youths unfamiliar with the sea, and he taught them how to live cleanly and tidily in the close quarters of a small ship. Shiner had served as a boy aboard the Hood, and had finished his second period of service when the war began. By the time that it was over—if he survived—he must have spent some twenty-eight years in the Navy.

Life aboard a great warship had its own special unity. Fleet regattas, sports, football, and boxing matches, all conspired to weld men into a dedication to their ship. Within the ship, of course, there were similar friendly rivalries which led to efficiency: the topmen, for instance, would always consider that they could manage all evolutions and drills more efficiently than fo'c's'lemen; the starboard watch that they could handle things better than the port; and the stokers that seamen were only carried aboard by courtesy of the engine-room staff. The Marines, somewhat naturally, considered that "Anything you can do we can do better." Overriding everything came the loyalty to the ship, so that a cap tally glimpsed ashore in some port or large city, bearing the name "H.M.S. Hood," meant not only a shipmate, but a friend.

By shoreside standards the sailor's life, whether he was officer or rating, might seem limited. They had their compensations, though, and they were many. "Come," wrote Corbière, "on board their ships they have their poetry!" and, when I think back on some of these men, I would echo another line of his:

> C'est plus qu'un homme aussi devant la mer géante,
> Ce matelot entier!

7

One Day in 1922

Imagine a soft day in the September of 1922. The coast of Brazil lies ahead, the Carioca mountains lifting out of the morning haze. Seen from this distance, the three peaks round which Rio de Janeiro is built have the shape of a sleeping giant. Dividing the white houses and the skyscrapers rises the peak known as The Hunchback. At the entrance to the bay the conical Sugar Loaf mountain needles the sky.

Six o'clock and the hands have just fallen in at their parts of ship. There is dew on the deck, for the humidity off this coast is high and the wind is drawing from the land—bringing with it a heavy smell of damp earth and tropical flowers, of heat and the city. Soon the steady trade winds will pick up with the day and begin to blow from astern, lifting the sea that has been with us all night and sending flickers of spray high over the long sheer of the quarterdeck. The Hood sits easily in a sea like this and the Atlantic swell does not bother her as it does the smaller ships.

"In the Hood," wrote one of her officers, "we don't feel the weather very much. She takes sixteen seconds in rolling her normal arc, whereas in the Atlantic and most oceans the period of roll is eleven seconds. The happy result is that our broad-beamed lady is little more than halfway through her roll when the next wave catches her and steadies her. I find all this very palatial after destroyers. . . . It's much the same when we have a head or a stern sea—the period between the average Atlantic wave crest is about 400 feet, but the fact that the Hood is over 800 feet long means she is always on two waves, or sometimes on three. . . . As you know," he went on, "we're on our way to Brazil for the centenary celebrations of their independence. We'll be there today—well, within a few hours; the coast is already in sight."

One thing you would notice is that, while the long fo'c's'le is completely dry, not a flicker of water reaching it, there are times when the stern settles down in a trough and seems to take a long time to rise. She was always wet aft in a big sea, and even the graceful sweep of her sheer—running upward all the way from "Y" turret to the ensign staff—could not keep her completely dry. The reason was not hard to find. When the alterations to her design had been made, and the extra armor added, she had floated some three feet deeper in the water than had originally been intended. This reduced freeboard was partially offset by the marked sheer at her bows and stern, but it was never enough to keep her quarterdeck dry in heavy weather.

Right up in the bows, standing between the great hawes-pipes and listening to the crunch and thunder of the broken sea under your feet, you got a true picture of the ship. She had that beautiful rakish clipper bow, with a big flare so that the razored waves were flung wide and clear. From the jackstaff, right in the eyes of her, you could see how the deck fell away in a graceful curve toward "A" turret, whose polished tampions gleamed in the early sun.

They were moving one of the guns now—up to its maximum elevation of 30 degrees. The turrets were unlike those in any previous ships. They could train 60 degrees abaft the beam, and had a flatter roof than on any previous British battleship. Five inches of armored steel covered the roof, there was 15-inch plating on the face, and the sides had a thickness of 11 to 12 inches. For the first time sighting hoods had been dispensed with and a 30-foot range finder spanned the top.

"B" turret rose behind "A" and then the dense steel cliffs of the bridge and the conning tower, with the sunlight shining on windows and apertures, and the flicker of small figures behind them. The conning tower was the heaviest and most elaborate that had been designed. There were 600 tons of armor on its more exposed sides. Above, on the crown, was the main gunnery control position with a 30-foot range finder moving in a revolving hood. She was the last British capital ship to have masthead control tops, but those giant steel nests, although old-fashioned, added to the strength and grandeur of her appearance.

She was also the last British warship to have a large secondary battery of twelve 5.5-inch guns, in open batteries. If you walked aft and climbed the ladders leading to the shelterdeck behind the bridge, you found the secondary batteries to port and starboard of the funnels. The shelterdeck ran scrubbed and shining past the two huge funnels (through either of them two London tube trains could have been driven abreast). Then you came to the boatdeck where eighteen boats ranging from 50-foot steam pinnaces to 16-foot dinghies were stowed. Rigged from the mainmast were the tackles leading to the derricks, and round the foot of the mast the first battery of 4-inch antiaircraft guns lifted their gray muzzles. Beyond that, and turning slowly against the skyline, was the secondary director, and then the torpedo control position. Searchlights opened blank eyes above this further mass of steel. At the very end of the shelterdeck was another battery of antiaircraft guns.

Looking down now from the break of the deck, the roof of "X" turret lay immediately below you and beyond it, half hidden from this angle, "Y" turret and the receding barrels of the guns. Then there was nothing but the salt-drenched sweep of the quarterdeck, and beyond that the marbled face of the Atlantic.

On deck you had the air of the moving sea, and that curious tang which haunts a big warship—a compound of metal polish, drying wood, new paint, caustic soda, and soap. Occasionally a hot brassy taste of funnel fumes would drop down under some errant air current, then the sea smell would come back clearer and cleaner, aided perhaps by the crisp scent of new bread rising from the bakery just forward of the secondary battery.

At nine o'clock, cleaned into the rig of the day, the ship's company fell in for "divisions" and prayers. Breakfast over, "divisions" was the formal routine inspection before the day's work was assigned. Prayers were held every day before the ship's activity was resumed. "Not like now," writes a retired petty officer, "when I see they've made Church Service optional in the fleet. We had prayers every morning. I think it was a good thing myself. Put us all, and the ship, in our proper perspective. Of course the Hood had her own chapel for Communion and Divine Service. We carried the fleet padre. I think she was the only ship in the fleet to have her own private chapel. . . ."

This afternoon in Rio de Janeiro the ship would be open to visitors. The chapel was one of the things they would probably see, but there was so much that they never would. She was so large that the average sailor knew little more of the ship than his own messdeck, his action station, his sea watch station, and the part of ship to which he was assigned. Down below, it was easy enough to lose your way. When visitors were aboard, messengers were stationed at various points to conduct them safely through each separate area, at the end of which the messenger handed over his charges to another. (It was likely that he would himself have got lost outside the section which he knew.)

Although the Hood had scuttles in a few places, it was mainly a world of electric light and forced ventilation in which you found yourself. Designed to live and fight in any quarter of the world, special attention had been paid to her ventilation, so that, closed up for action whether in tropic or arctic conditions, her crew could still work their ship efficiently. Engine and boiler rooms had their natural supply, but the rest of the ship was served by supply and exhaust fans. The low-pressure air purred through long miles of trunking—the steady background noise that became part of the sailors' silence. Now, in these warm waters, the air was the same temperature as outside, but had they been in polar regions it would have been warmed before circulating through the ship. To insure that none of the main bulkheads were pierced and weakened by the fan trunkings, each of the main transverse compartments had its own air supply. Below water she was divided into five hundred watertight compartments.

Half of a sailor's time is spent in housemaid's work, and, like all ships, the Hood needed constant attention. Like the Forth Bridge, no sooner was an operation such as painting one side of the ship completed, than the other side must be started. Plumbing, lighting, galley maintenance, rust prevention, and just plain cleaning were chores that never ceased.

"Join the Navy and see the world!" was the sailor's moan, his face a yard or so away from the bulkhead he was cleaning, a piece of waste in his hand, and a bucket of "strongers"—hot water, caustic soda, and soap—at his feet. ("I'll still be down 'ere scrubbing this galley flat when they 'angs 'Itler!" I remember one sour veteran saying in later days.)

There was more bright work then than now. From binnacles, compass rings, telescope bands, brass rails, brass-mounted tillers, and metal treads on ladders, innumerable pinpoints of light flickered against the warship's dreadnought gray.

Overalls rolled down to the waist, two stokers were checking the capstan grease points in the capstan flat under the fo'c's'le. In the next compartment aft lay the trim, empty operating theater. A sick berth attendant looked in for a moment, checked that everything was in its proper place, and closed the door behind him. Farther aft under the turret of "A" gun was the sick bay itself, with five cots occupied. Aft again, and under "B" turret, the petty officers' reading room lay empty save for one sailor scrubbing the deck. Next to it in the petty officers' mess there was the cheerful clatter of pots and pans where the messman was polishing the utensils for the midday meal. The "spitkids," large circular bowls dating back to the days when sailors chewed their tobacco and spat in a way that would now earn them punishment, shone as bright as silver and pooled the scrubbed deck with light. Now they were used as ash trays, and the messman who polished them every day always felt a pang when the first cigarettes dropped into them at the midmorning "stand easy."

The sea boat's crew was being exercised, a routine that took place every watch. A midshipman and a lieutenant were checking the evolution, the midshipman with a stop watch in his hand.

"Half a minute slower than last time, sir," he announced.

"Not good." The lieutenant turned to the petty officer in charge. "Still the slowest. If there was a man in the water, every second would count—"

"Yessir. New coxswain, sir. Jackson's gone sick." The men secured the boat, nattering to each other.

"What you want to get them gripes all fouled up for?"

"Never even shipped the tiller."

"Not bleeding quick enough, 'e says."

At all levels the ship was busy—one deck down, two decks down, deep under water, in her communicating passages, her offices, stores, galleys, her boiler rooms, and her engine rooms.

Below the fo'c's'le lay the carpenter's workshop—Chippy's shop—resinous with the scent of pine shavings. A new strake was being made for one of the boats. Pale, floating flakes of wood lifted in front of the plane as Chippy's assistant fined down the entrance of the long plank. A pot of glue bubbled in the corner. Through the steel bulkhead behind the carpenter's store came the murmur of machinery, broken every now and then by the high moan of a thread being cut in a steel bolt. That was the artificers' workshop: a world of spinning lathes, coiled springlike piles of metal shavings, and the bitter smell of sharpened steel.

Below the artificers' workshop lay the launderers' store; gleaming sheets, napkins, tablecloths, and pillow slips. The admiral's steward was drawing enough fresh table linen to last him through the round of dinner parties and entertainments that lay ahead. In the passage outside, and a little forward of the launderers' store, sailors were unclipping a watertight door leading down to one of the ship's many provision stores. A lieutenant stood back, waiting for them and consulting a check list in his hand. Seven thousand pounds of fresh meat and 12,600 pounds of fresh vegetables would have to be embarked at Rio. He had just remembered that there were not enough tins of cocktail biscuits, almonds, and olives in the wardroom cupboard for the cocktail party to be given that night.

On deck two sailors lurked in the lee of a boat and looked at the land ahead.

"Been 'ere before, ain't you, Stripey?" asked the younger.

"Lots of times. Got me feet under the table 'ere. You see—my party'll be down to pick me up in 'er motor car. Irish-Spanish she is. Widow. I'm thinking of settlin' out 'ere when me time's up. She's got a department store—always a job there for *me*, she says."

Department store! thought the other. If he was going out with a barmaid, he'd say she owned the brewery.

The steady sea wind had already overridden the land breeze, and the hoist of flags that lifted to the main yard hung irresolute for a moment between the wind of the ship's movement and this new wind from astern. Telegraphs clanged in the engine room and, within a few minutes, the bright arrow of her wake began to fade and turn into a gentle swath as the speed came down. The other ships in company acknowledged the order and executed it as the flag hoist dropped from Hood's yardarm.

In his day cabin Rear-Admiral Sir Walter Cowan was discussing with his chief-of-staff and his secretary the arrangements made for the reception and formalities at Rio. The captain was on the bridge, the squadron navigating officer beside him. Hood began to swing gently through the water, as she altered course one point to starboard for her approach course to the great bay. The fort of Santa Cruz one one side of the entrance and the fort of São João on the other were quite distinct now under binoculars. Between them the mile-wide channel ran blue and clear, save for a single-funneled merchant ship trailing a snail's track across the water. Her smoke rose up in a dark thread, vertical against the green of the land: no wind in the bay. The onshore breeze lifted before the city and went up high over the hills.

Along the docks and crowding thick on the foreshore people were already gathering, their eyes turned seaward. There she came! Breasting out of the simple blue of the Atlantic, she raised her bows and battlements—a cloud no bigger than a man's hand —the Hood.

8

Start of the World Cruise

The idea of a world cruise by a heavy British squadron had been under consideration for some time. The war had been over five years, and the world was reshaping into new power blocs. Everywhere the conditions of life were changing. Many people in the British colonies and Dominions had never seen the fleet, or any of the capital ships, upon which their safety and their lives had depended between 1914 and 1918. The sea lanes and the communications, behind which South Africa, Australia, and Canada had grown up into young giants, had been maintained and patrolled almost entirely by the Royal Navy. Yet, except for an occasional visit by a flotilla of light ships or a passing cruiser, the people of these countries had never been able to see or judge for themselves the nature of their defense.

In 1922 consultations were held between the governors and cabinets of the Dominions, the governors of colonies and foreign protectorates, the Admiralty, and the Foreign Office. Their conclusion was that it would be a wise cementing of old friendships to send an important British squadron round the world. They planned that the ships would call formally on the Dominions, colonies, and protectorates. Such a gesture of showing the flag would fulfill two purposes: it would strengthen the links of the

Commonwealth at every level, and it would serve to remind the peoples of the new countries that the price of Admiralty was a heavy one. It had been paid in blood during the recent war, but it was also economically heavy in the depressed postwar era. Nearly all the burden was borne by the British taxpayer.

King George V was a keen supporter of the scheme. A sailor at heart, he was never happier than when aboard his racing cutter Britannia. He was also an enthusiast for anything that, as well as binding together his Empire, served to promote the interests of the Navy. Had it been possible he would undoubtedly have gone on the cruise himself.

A rigid disciplinarian, and a man who could be stern enough if need be, the King was not without a sense of humor. A letter written by one of his junior officers at this time read: ". . . As you know, I'll be off in 'The Mighty 'ood' on this world cruise very soon. From the little that the sec. has told me about the programme, it looks as if it will turn out to be a 'World Booze' as well. Dances, parties, and so-on at every port we visit." The King would probably have laughed if he had seen it.

The ships, their officers and men, destined for the cruise, were all carefully chosen. As the most improtant unit of British sea power, it was natural that the Hood should be picked to lead the squadron. The Repulse, a fine example of a conventional battle cruiser, was to accompany her, together with the First Light Cruiser Squadron, H.M. ships Delhi, Dauntless, Danae, Dragon, and Dunedin. In command of the whole operation, aboard the Hood, was Vice-Admiral Sir Frederic Laurence Field, K.C.B., C.M.G. Rear-Admiral the Honorable Sir Hubert Brand, K.C.M.G., K.C.V.O., C.B., was Rear-Admiral commanding the Light Cruiser Squadron. The ships would leave England in November 1923, and it was expected that they would be away for nearly a year.

No British squadron since the days of sail had made a voyage round the world, and it cannot have been without a sense of the historic nature of the occasion that Admiral Field made his first report to the Admiralty: "I have the honour to report that I proceeded from Devonport in H.M.S. Hood with H.M. ships Delhi and Dauntless at 0700 on 27th November. . . ." On a cold Channel day the ships swept down toward the Eddystone Lighthouse, where the Repulse and the other cruisers joined them. The squadron was now complete, and course was set for the first port of call, Freetown in Sierra Leone.

His Majesty the King signaled them just before they left English waters: "On the eve of your departure on the Empire cruise I wish you, the officers and ships' companies of the squadron, a happy, successful voyage and safe return; my thoughts and good wishes will always be with you." It was the beginning of the most successful cruise by a squadron of warships in the history of sea power. There was never one like it before, and there will never be another.

The weather in the Bay of Biscay was fine for the time of year. No gales swept the squadron as they made their way down from the cold north to southern latitudes. Only the eternal heave and swell of the great ocean, as it ran on to the continental shelf, reminded them that this was the bay "unkind to seafarers." A hundred years earlier Lord Byron on his way to Gibraltar had commented on "Biscay's sleepless bay." The same heavy swell which left the Hood almost undisturbed made the light cruisers roll upward of 20 degrees each way.

Soon they were down in "flying-fish weather." The wakes at night were shining pathways of phosphorescence, and before their bows the flying fish rose and soared in flickering silver showers. Dancing and turning just ahead of the broken water at Hood's forefoot, the porpoises rolled and played—a source of endless fascination to the sailors. The snorting fish lifted always a few inches clear of the knife edge of steel, and were never cut down by the lean bows.

Admiral Field was to prove himself on this cruise one of the best ambassadors Britain ever had. He was a better ambassador for the reason that, as a naval officer, he was necessarily uninvolved in politics. His tact, discretion, and ability to make the right speech in the right place were invaluable assets. Without them the cruise might well have failed in its major aim: that of consolidating old friendships and making new ones.

His abilities were put to the test almost as soon as the squadron reached its first port of call. He quickly noted that in a community like Freetown, where the population was a mixture of European and African, there must inevitably be many jealousies. By carefully balancing the entertainments and the receptions, the Admiral managed to leave both sections pleased and flattered. It was no small feat. Here, as elsewhere, he was immediately ready to ascribe most of the success of the visit to the good behavior of the ships' companies. "There was not one case of leave breaking in the whole squadron."

In Freetown Hood was presented with the first of many trophies with which she was to be inundated before the cruise was over—an elephant's tusk mounted in silver and given her by the city council. Thousands lined the shores of the steamy African port as she put to sea, the native boats gradually dropping astern as she gathered way, their bronze-skinned divers plunging over the sides of their canoes for the last coin flung by the sailors. In the Nelson bar they were tacking up a photograph of the ship which would still be there (sepia-colored and fly-specked) twenty years later. Already a legend was being born.

A few days out from Freetown the squadron crossed the line. Father Neptune's court ceremonially invaded each vessel on a day of bright sunshine and puffy trade-wind clouds. The ships were making 16 knots, the cruisers disposed abeam to starboard of the battle cruisers, and the long South Atlantic swell was beginning to lift under their sterns. A thousand men aboard Hood were new to the freedom of the southern seas, and Neptune's court was busy with all the ritual of razors and soap, and the ceremonial ducking of the initiates.

Apart from such age-old traditions that centuries of British men-of-war had carried out crossing the equator, the ships were busy carrying out gunnery exercises and action drills. In those immediate postwar years one of the future hazards that had to be reckoned with was the use of gas. The horror of gas attacks on the western front in France had stamped itself on people's imaginations. Gas shells had never been used at sea in any engagements between the British and German fleets, but it was thought that, in the event of another war, gas shells might well be used to wipe out guns' crews, bridge personnel, and exposed positions. Gas bombs dropped by aircraft were another possibility. Hood had been designed with this danger in view and, while the ships rolled down to South Africa, they carried out exercises to test the efficiency of the antigas precautions.

Hood's transmitting station was sealed from natural air ventilation, and gunnery firing practice was carried out. In the event, it was proved that within a very short time the humidity of this nerve center of the ship rose to 90 degrees and conditions were soon impossible for the crew. One officer collapsed with heat stroke. Gas was never used at sea in World War II, any more than it was on land. It is worth recording that in the early 1920's, when many critics were saying that the Navy lived in the past, and that capital ships were antediluvian mammoths, the potential avenues of new types of attack were being tested and explored.

As the ships entered the approaches to Table Bay the weather closed down. The South Atlantic rolled up one of its dense sea fogs, and the ships streamed fog buoys to enable their next astern to maintain course and station. The fog buoy is a simple floatlike device, streamed over the quarter and designed to kick up the maximum amount of wash in the water. It is run out on a wire hawser to the required length, so as to insure a safe maneuvering distance between the warships. The lookouts and the officers of the watch on the following ship keep their eyes on the tumbling white foam of the buoy. In the days before radar there was no other way of keeping a fleet in contact at close distance during thick weather.

Opinions ashore were divided as to the visit. South Africans of British stock were delighted that such a display of Empire strength was being made, but it was significant that the Afrikaans newspapers pointedly ignored the squadron. Any reminder that the prosperity of South Africa was dependent upon the Royal Navy was not to their liking. It was difficult for them to forget that the potentialities of Table Bay had first been noted by the Dutch East Indiamen, and it was Dutch ships which had first made of this great harbor, and of the fertile land behind it, a victualing depot and a repair point. Out of this maritime establishment had evolved the Dutch expansion throughout the Cape colony, and it was not until the close of the eighteenth century that the British had landed an army to secure the Cape against the French. They had never left. Now, their ships were here to remind the old settler stock that the sea lanes to the colony were kept open only by the British fleet. It was in situations like this that all the tact of Admiral Field and his companion Admiral Brand was needed.

It was late December when the squadron secured in Table Bay. The weather had lifted, but the heavy swell of the southeasters which poured into the bay made the reception and embarkation of guests a hazardous operation. Important guests tend to be, as the Admiral remarked, "all oldish men." Transporting them and landing them safely on the warship's gangway kept the deck officer's heart in his mouth, and the midshipmen at the tillers of the boats apprehensive and clammy-handed. Despite the bad weather and the difficulty of carrying so many guests out to a ship at anchor, 17,000 people visited the Hood while she lay in Table Bay. There were no accidents.

It was now Christmas, and there must have been some fear that thousands of sailors ashore in a new country, with an unfamiliar climate and unfamiliar drinks (like the throat-searing Cape brandy) might lead to trouble and disorder. Yet, after the ships left, the chief of the Cape Town police reported that he had ". . . never known a Christmas or New Year so free from any signs of rowdyism in the native quarters." He attributed this to the good example set by the many sailors ashore, and to the imposing dignity of the march through the city of nine hundred sailors and marines, preceded by the marine band. Such ceremonial marches were a part and parcel of the ship's visit to every new city and port.

The long gray-white cloud, known as the "tablecloth," was streaming off the shoulders of the great mountain as the ships weighed and set course up the South African coast. The Dutch press might have been silent about the visit, but the comments of the English-language newspapers showed that the purpose of the cruise was already being achieved. The *Cape Times* pointed out:

> This is the most valuable lesson for those in South Africa who cherish the Republican Hope. The Fool's Paradise of a Republic immune from foreign interference that the Nationalists have built in their imagination is shattered by the mere presence of these warships in Table Bay. Perhaps that is why the Dutch press has been blind to and dumb about them. It might be inconvenient to reflect that other powers than Great Britain have warships afloat.

Nearly forty years later the comment is still apt. The presence of the Hood and Repulse had also achieved recognition of the fact that. . . . "For good or ill the superdreadnought remains—at any rate for some time to come—the foundation of Sea Power."

It was something of an achievement at any rate that, in a city where the quality of the fleet's welcome had been somewhat doubtful to begin with, a huge crowd gathered to watch them leave. It was significant that many in the crowd were singing that old music hall song which had marked the high tide of pre-1914 patriotism:

> The foe may build the ships, my lads,
> And think they know the game;
> But they can't beat the boys of the bulldog breed
> That made old England's name.

9

"Leviathans Revealed . . ."

By the time the squadron reached Fremantle, some three months later, what had started as an experiment in Empire relations and an exercise in training men and ships, had become a triumphal procession.

> Half moon among the stars; the sea whipped by a land wind; clusters of lights on the horizon north of Rottnest; lights drawing nearer and nearer; green flares rising and falling; lights dimmed by dawn; lights no longer errant, unattached, but seen as multitudinous eyes upon vague, grey shapes; dawn limning the shapes as ships; Leviathans revealed. . . .

A hard-bitten Australian journalist found poetic prose coming from his typewriter. He went on to record his first impressions of the flagship:

> . . . No ship of war "with castled stern and lanterned poop" is the Hood. The picturesque has yielded to the terrible. Her mailed might appals and exalts—appals because of her sheer size and strength of armament; exalts because, in her, England is still England.

After leaving Cape Town the squadron had visited Port Elizabeth, East London, and Durban, before running north up the African coast to visit the island of Zanzibar. Zanzibar, with its humid climate, its strange red soil, and luxuriant vegetation was then, as now, the world's greatest producer of cloves. If the wind was offshore you could smell the damp soil, the cloves, and the tropical flowers, many miles out at sea. During the war, the old British cruiser Pegasus had been surprised in Zanzibar roadstead by the German Königsberg and sunk in full view of the island. For this reason, apart from any other, it was thought that the sight of the Hood and her sister ships would dispel any local doubts as to whose was the final victory.

Sayid Khalifa ben Hamid, the Sultan of Zanzibar, received the Admiral aboard the government dispatch vessel. The party then drove to the palace for the formal dinner and reception. They went through hot, narrow streets smelling of cloves, where only the crests of the palm trees were stirred by the monsoon winds. The winding alleys were decorated with flags, and noisy with the cries of Arabs, Hindus, Persians, Goanese, Parsis, and Swahili; the confettilike pattern of race and language that matches the exotic nature of the island. It was here that the local Arab Society came forward with a welcoming address:

"We heartily congratulate Your Excellency on the unique honor of being in command of the largest battle cruiser in the world. . . . We hope and trust that His Majesty's Government will continue to protect the interests of the Arabs of this part of the world."

It was an example of the clemency of British rule that, although the island had originally been a sultanate deriving from the Imams of Muscat, no attempt had ever been made to eradicate Arab influence after Zanzibar had come under British protection. It was rather the reverse, in fact, and the rights and religious practices of the Arabs had been as carefully safeguarded as those of the native Bantus. In our day "imperialism" has become a bad word. History may judge differently. The world cruise of a ship like the Hood may be seen in its true perspective, as the benevolent gesture of a safeguarding power—unlike the tanks that "protect" the security of countries such as Hungary today.

From Zanzibar the squadron turned east, and headed across the Indian Ocean for Trincomalee in Ceylon. The northeast monsoon was blowing, a steady force five to six, day after day. The palm trees on the coral islands of the Maldive group bent before the prevailing wind. Every now and then the squadron steamed through a tropical downpour, the rain beating like thunder on their steel decks. The warm water seemed to steam as the raindrops whipped the surface like sand shot.

From Ceylon they ran on down to Singapore, where the new naval base was under construction, and where the first casualty of the cruise occurred. An able seaman from Hood died of malaria at Port Swettenham. Visiting Selangor, the Admiral and his officers were entertained at the Confucian School to a Chinese banquet. The menu would have cheered the heart of a world-weary Manchu Emperor:

Grilled Shark Fins
Bird's Nest Soup
Iced Chicken and Ham
(with Oriental salad)
Grilled Awabi
Fried Oysters on Toast
Omelette
Toefoo Custard
Dessert and Souchong Tea

Out of training, perhaps, after the simplicities of sea life, Admiral Field and several of his officers were ill with sore throats as the ships turned south for Australia! The Admiral's sore throat may have been due to other causes than the unfamiliar Chinese food, for in Singapore he had to make two or three speeches a day, as well as give interviews to the press. Among certain sections of the colony there was deep opposition to the new naval base. It was openly said that Singapore had now been turned into a pistol pointing at the heart of Japan, and that the Japanese could not fail to see it as such. Subsequent events proved this view only too correct, but it was the Admiral's task to try and allay such fears. It is possible he may himself have felt that a naval base of such importance would have been better established in Australia (an opinion loudly voiced by Australian politicians and sections of the press at this time). If so, he concealed his feelings, parried the criticisms directed against the Singapore dockyard project, and left the various sections of the community, if not at ease, at least less worried than they had been before the squadron's arrival. (If the money spent on the Singapore dockyard had been spent on a similar project in Australia, the course of World War II in the Far East might have been very different.)

The Australian reception of the squadron was tumultuous, ecstatic; something that people in Fremantle, Melbourne, Perth, and Hobart still talk about. The advent of the ships coincided with Australia's new sense of herself as a growing country, with a large stake in the future. It was the first time that the friendly, openhearted Australians had had a chance to see the great ships about which they had heard so much. It was a chance for many of them to renew old friendships formed with the Navy in the Dardanelles and other theaters of World War I.

The Hood was the focus of attention. Every move and activity aboard her was watched by dozens of reporters circling round her in motorboats. As soon as the official reception was over and the Admirals had gone ashore, one Fremantle journalist noted that the sailors "set to cleaning their ship, polishing and painting, while those who were not on duty leant over the sides and whistled at the pretty girls in our boat." He remarked that: "Several motor cars are carried aboard her, including the Admiral's Rolls Royce. All of these were quickly disembarked." Today, it is common enough for large warships to land motorized patrols, but the Hood was probably the first ship to carry her own motor transport. The Rolls Royce itself lends the flavor of a more sumptuous and "jeepless" age.

The *Western Australian* interviewed Admiral Field in his day cabin and commented:

> In its space and appointments and quietness there is nothing to distinguish it from an apartment in some luxurious city hotel—nothing, that is to say, but the occasional piping of a whistle or the faint echo of a smartly rapped-out order overhead. In the adjoining room, with its dining accommodation for thirty-five or thirty-six persons, the mahogany furniture was matched by two mantelpieces enclosing capacious grates designed for coal fires.

He remarked on the ornaments on the mantelpieces, and the absence of any "fiddles" or retaining pieces for glasses, photographs, and china. The Admiral told him that, except in very heavy weather, the ship's motion was so easy such things were unnecessary. Field's charm and easy manner endeared him to the press as much as to the official reception committees. "Many of the published photographs of Admiral Field are libellous. One expected to meet a man of sunken cheeks and world-weary eyes. Instead one was confronted with a cheery countenance—bright alert eyes and a twinkle of humour in them."

At Melbourne the city went mad.

> . . . I was a girl of eighteen at the time and I remember quite clearly my father taking us all out to Port Phillip Heads to see the squadron come in. It was early March and glorious weather. There were thousands of other people up with us. Every road and pathway was thick and many families were making a day of it, taking out all the children and hampers of food and bottles of beer. The Bay was dotted with sailing boats. Everyone who had anything that would float—big yachts to small rowing boats—was out there on the water. It was hot and very still, and at sea there was a white sea mist. I believe the papers said there were 500,000 people waiting to see the ships. "Here they come!" said my father, and then we could hear the aircraft. It was a wonderful sight—something I can never forget. The mist out at sea, and then the aircraft coming through it, and then a few minutes later the Hood herself, with the white cloud seeming to peel away from her as she came on into the bright sunlight of Port Phillip.

> Everyone cheering and the kids running up and down and the sirens of all the ships in the harbour going off—

It had been the same at Albany and Adelaide. When they left the latter, the weather had been perfect, with a light heat haze lying over the water. The *Advertiser* had reported their departure:

> The sea as calm as a mill pond. The pinnaces from the cruisers at the jetty at an early hour, gathering up final supplies, mails and papers. . . . At 9.15 the light cruisers, which had cast off from the wharfs at the outer harbour, were picked up 4 or 5 miles in the offing, lying almost hull down in the horizon, and appearing like ghost ships as they leaned through the light haze. The winking of a signal lamp on one of the distant craft elicited answering flashes from high up in the superstructure of the Hood, and in a few minutes the water began to churn beneath her stern. The flagship of the Special Service Squadron moved out into the waters of the gulf. With the bright rays of the sun glinting on her brass-work and throwing into relief the grim turrets and guns, set off by the regulation dreadnought grey, she furnished a never-to-be-forgotten sight as she sped away with all the grace of a launch. Scarcely less majestic was the Repulse which followed a few cable lengths astern. Thousands along the foreshore, from the Outer Mole to Marino, watched the grey hulls as they gradually grew less and less and finally faded away into the haze. . . .

At very port of call there were sports events against local teams, ceremonial marches through the cities, and as well as official dinners and banquets there were dances, cocktail parties, and open-air barbecues. At Melbourne the same young lady recalls a dance given by the junior officers.

> . . . I and my elder sister were both invited. People sometimes talk about the first big dance that a young girl goes to, but I think no one could have had a more wonderful time than I did. Dinner was at half-past seven, I think, and before that we had champagne. Champagne seemed to "go with" the ship somehow and I never drink it now without remembering the Hood. At that time I had never tasted it before. I remember my sister telling me not

> to have more than one glass! Then there was the dance on the quarterdeck. They had a squadron song, I am afraid I have forgotten it. . . . I remember sitting on one of the turrets of the big guns, there was a whole group of us and a young lieutenant with a ukulele, he was playing the tune and the others were singing.

The song they were singing was:

> Oh, oh, oh, the S.S.S.
> There never was a squadron like the S.S.S.
> North, South, East and West
> We'll show the world we're better than their best.
> All Australia visited the Hood,
> But they couldn't sink her, nobody could.
> There never was a squadron like the S.S.S.

The cheerful braggadocio of the words echoes down the years. The young lieutenant with the ukulele, and the young girl whose first big party it was, are figures preserved forever in the bright amber of the passing moment.

"Gangway, please, let the girl see the big gun!" was the cry as the guests were ferried ashore. At Perth a correspondent to the local paper confirmed the opinion of the young girl at Melbourne ". . . But to be filled with the joy of life and to experience the exhilaration of the dance one must accompany the lieutenants and midshipmen. . . . Cocktails, champagne and liqueurs started things going!"

It was at this moment that in America the magazine *Scientific American* was rash enough to publish the statement that the U.S.S. Colorado was the largest battleship afloat. The Australian press, primed with data, sprang to battle and compared the dimensions of the Hood with the Colorado.

> Our American friends need to get their facts right:

	COLORADO	HOOD
Length	624′	810′
Beam	97′	104′

	COLORADO	HOOD
Draught	31′	28½′
Tons	32,600	41,200
Speed	21 knots	32 knots
Armament	8—16″	8—15″
Subsidiary Armament	12—5″	12—5.5″
	8—3″	4—4″
		4—3 pounders
Torpedoes	2—21″ submerged	2—21″ submerged
		4—21″ above water line
Complement	1,410	1,443

The fact was that the Colorado certainly carried a heavier main armament, but Australia was in no mood at that moment to accept the suggestion that there could be any ship in the world to compare with the "Mighty Hood." At every port, more trophies and more mascots joined the ship. A number of parrots were easy enough to house, but one wonders what happened to the kangaroo that was formally presented in Adelaide.

Everywhere the sailors were welcome and popular. It was not surprising that, with Australia crying out for young immigrants and offering them many inducements, a few of the sailors deserted. It was not only the lure of a new and rich country that attracted the adventurous:

> . . . There is no doubt the sprinkling of uniforms of the sailors about the streets during the last few days has gone a long way towards brightening up the city [Adelaide]. At any rate the ladies appear to think so, for it is very noticeable that every tar has his admirers among the fair sex, and the undisguised glances of admiration that follow the men in blue as they stroll unconcernedly down the streets would turn the heads of many older men less used to being the cynosure of all eyes.

As the Hood left Melbourne, a broad web of colored streamers was spun between the flagship and the pier, officers and men holding one end of the paper streamers—"frail link with the friends they were leaving behind." The twisting colored ribbons grew longer and longer, rainbow bright in the early sunlight, and then trailed broken in the water as the battle cruiser crept out to sea.

The Admiral and his company could congratulate themselves on one of the most successful visits in history. The attitude of the Australian press was summed up by the editorial of the Melbourne *Sun.*

> To say that Australia was cradled in the strong arms of the British Navy is more than a figure of speech. It was the command of the seas that made a British Australia possible. It is due to British sea power that Australia is the only continent that has never had to suffer an invasion. . . .

There was only one dissentient voice. If it is worth quoting today, it is only because it faithfully reflected the attitude of Labour throughout the interwar years, both in Australia and in Great Britain. Frank Cotton in the *Australian Worker* wrote: "The amount of money expended in building a battleship like the Hood would have built 10,000 comfortable cottages for British one-room slum dwellers. The idea that a state of military or naval preparedness is any factor in the security of a nation is A MYTH THAT HAS LONG SINCE BEEN EXPLODED." The capitals are Mr. Cotton's.

10

To the New World

In Hobart, Tasmania, 42,000 people visited the Hood. More than 100,000 went aboard the other ships of the squadron.

"By rail, steamer and coaches," said the local newspaper, "people have thronged the city from all parts of the island to see England's mighty ships."

Here as elsewhere the local police chief reported that, despite the hundreds of British sailors ashore in the city, there had been no trouble or disturbance. In Melbourne, the commissioner of police had gone so far as to say: "The British sailor ashore behaved like a gentleman. Far from being able to teach him anything in the way of manners or sobriety, a big portion of Melbourne had something to learn from him."

On leaving Australia the Special Service Squadron took with them the newly commissioned Australian cruiser H.M.A.S. Adelaide. Apart from the benefit of training with units of the fleet, the Adelaide was a good advertisement of Australian participation in Empire defense. Her presence in the squadron was to make a profound impression in Canada. Since one of the purposes of the cruise was to make the Dominions and colonies aware of the necessity of contributing to the defense of the

British Empire, the Adelaide's part in the second half of the world cruise was important. In New Zealand the Dunedin was formally transferred to the New Zealand division, and another stone was thus laid in the defenses of the Dominions.

The New Zealanders gave the squadron a welcome that equaled that of Australia. In Wellington, in the space of four days, over 78,000 people visited the Hood. Here, as in Melbourne, she became a legend.

In Alexandria, in 1941, I met a New Zealand sergeant, on leave from the Western Desert, who recalled being taken as a small boy aboard Hood by his father.

"My old man," he said, "had got me a sailor suit for the occasion. They've still got the picture of me in it at home, taken the day when we went aboard. It makes my kids laugh—you don't see sailor suits now like you used to then. I remember the *matelots* had got the main capstan on the foredeck rigged up as a merry-go-round. There was a big fellow with a black beard standing in the middle of it, leading hand I think he was, keeping an eye on us to see no one fell off. That was a great time in Wellington. My old man and Mum had come in from thirty miles out, bringing the six of us with them. At night they had the ships all lit up and the Hood's searchlights playing about the sky. . . ."

Nearly 1,500 miles north of Auckland lie the Fiji Islands, a British colony and the most important archipelago in Polynesia. It was clearly impossible for the squadron to visit more than a section of the British possessions in the Pacific (the New Hebrides, the Gilbert and Ellice Islands, and the Solomon group alone being spread over thousands of miles of ocean). As the most important island in the major protectorate, however, it had been decided to visit Viti Levu and its capital Suva. After days on the long slow roll of the Pacific, where the limitless sea moves like an undulating field (a field that has once been plowed and then for many years left to grass), the ships sighted cumulus clouds hovering over the heads of the islands.

> . . . For sheer beauty I remember Suva in Fiji better than anywhere else on the cruise [wrote one officer]. Unlike most of the smaller islands, which are coral atolls, Suva is volcanic, with high peaks 3,000 to 4,000 feet high. Densely wooded, with lovely clear streams falling down through tangles of tropical flowers and shrubs. I think if I had had a bit more of the beachcomber's temperament I would have retired there. . . .

The islands had been ceded to Britain in 1874. One of the first tasks of the occupying power had been to stamp out the cannibalism which was prevalent among the islanders. It was almost their only vice, for in other respects the Fijians were the aristocrats of the Pacific. Their women were better treated than those among most Polynesians. They cultivated the arts and were fine potters. The craft of carpentry was so respected that it had become a hereditary caste, and their lattice-and-thatch houses were well built and attractively decorated. Their 100-foot-long canoes were magnificent sea boats.

In Fiji cannibalism had been a major problem. It had originated, perhaps, as a ritual, but by the time the British arrived human flesh had become a luxurious necessity. "Long pig," as the Fijians euphemistically called human flesh, was essential for any banquet. Cannibalism had been stamped out fifty years or more before the Hood and her squadron stood in out of the blue haze of the Pacific. But it is just possible that, among the thousands of natives who gathered to watch the "long ships," there were some who remembered the taste of human flesh. There may even have been one or two who remembered how in the old days, when they themselves were going to launch a new war canoe, it was over human rollers lashed between two plantain trees that the fighting vessel first took the sea and received its baptism of blood.

Here, in the islands where Lieutenant Bligh in the launch of the Bounty had been driven off by hostile natives, the Fijians received the sailors with hospitality. They even revived for their benefit the traditional fire-walking ceremony.

> . . . It was impossible to tell how it was done, whether by some self-induced indifference to pain (like the Indian fakirs) or because the soles of their feet could, for a few seconds, stand the intense heat. It was intense all right. Near the pit through which the chosen veterans walked, the air was quivering and you couldn't get close without flinching from the heat of the fire. They flicked long damp leaves over the hot stones before they walked across the pit, and the steam shot up like a burst boiler.

There were what the sailors called "banyan" parties—excursions to the beach, swimming, and sailing. They drank beer at long tables set out under the wind-bent palms, and bought native curios (later to grow dusty in a thousand homes from Portsmouth to Aberdeen). They watched the Fijians, agile as porpoises and almost as native to the sea, spearing fish in the shallows, or riding through the long breakers where the glistening noonday surf fetched up on the coral reefs. In those warm islands the ocean seems to lean against the land. They were sorry to see the humped peaks, the coral atolls, and the ever-green shadows drop astern.

Northward across the Pacific, the squadron moved on to Apia in Western Samoa, and closed the shore to allow the Governor to come aboard. They did not stay. They were bound now for the New World and their first visit to American waters.

It was the time when the Puritan conscience was trying to sweep "the demon drink" out of America. The country and all its possessions were declared "dry," and only the bootlegger rejoiced. Admiral Field was set with a nice problem—should he maintain the traditional hospitality of the Royal Navy, or should he, when in American waters, conform to the customs of his hosts? He decided that rather than risk giving any offense he would close all wardroom bars during the squadron's stay in Honolulu. His action was appreciated by the American authorities and, as one of them said, ". . . It also prevents your ships being thronged by thirsty residents—who are eager not so much to see the efficiency of the British fleet as to get a free drop of Scotch."

The Admiral's flair for making those small gestures which mean so much was revealed in the incident of Tom Frazier. A fifteen-year-old Boy Scout who had been selected to represent Hawaii at the International Assembly of Scouts in Copenhagen, Frazier had been unable to catch the routine steamer connection for America. There were no other ships leaving in time. Hearing of this, Admiral Field immediately suggested that the young scout should be given a passage in the Hood, and be accommodated in the boys' messdeck. It was a small action, but one which Hawaiian and American papers quickly noted: ". . . Scout Frazier not only gets to the Scout Assembly, but he gets there with a free passage in the world's mightiest warship."

The Admiral's popularity had never been in doubt, but it was gestures like this which endeared him not only to his own officers and men, but to outsiders and foreign visitors. When the ships finally reached Vancouver a reporter from the *Daily Province* quizzed some of the ship's company about the cruise and about their Admiral.

> I asked a great, hairy-chested, flat-nosed, bulldog type of seaman, who hailed from Devonport, what he and his comrades thought of the Admiral. He spat prodigiously over the ship's side and reflected a moment—
>
> "Guv'nor, 'e's just a British sailor—a gentleman. I can't say no more—and I don't need to. 'E's it!"
>
> An officer to whom I addressed the same question replied:
>
> "Everybody loves him. And, moreover, he has proved himself a really great man."

Between Honolulu, Victoria, and Vancouver, nearly a quarter of a million people had visited the ships. When they turned their bows southward toward San Francisco the Americans awaited them with the kind of welcome that even a visiting sovereign rarely receives. On July 10, 1924, the New York *Herald Tribune* reporter watched them stand in from sea.

> In a blare of whistles and saluting cannon seven men-of-war steam through the Golden Gate and come to anchor in San Francisco Harbor. The Admiral, in a profound deference to the inexplicable peculiarity of our institutions, commands that no rum is to be served out during the three days of the visit; and one senses the magnificence of the gesture, for his flag is hoisted in H.M.S. Hood, the most powerful ship of the British Navy. San Francisco reports that this is the first important British squadron to anchor in an American harbor for forty years. . . . They [the British and American] are the world's two most powerful navies, and the two of the very few that are certain never to be used against each other.

San Francisco, the famous seaport known to generations of old-time square-rigged seamen; Frisco, which had once boasted the toughest dockland in the world, showed its Janus face to the "limey" sailors. Its white skyscrapers, rapidly rising against the braced arms of the hills, contrasted with the noise and blare of the honky-tonk cabarets along Chinatown. American hospitality, despite the official "dry" nature of the times, was as generous and as warmhearted as ever—it is certain that the "liquor laws" were broken on a number of occasions.

The mayor of the city, in his welcoming address, set the tone for the whole reception:

"Your presence with us today will, we trust, make a pact between the English-speaking races even closer. We take a pride in your magnificent ships, which we feel will never be used except in the defense of the world's peace. We surrender our city unto you. We capitulate."

A pleasanter tribute than this, from the mayor of an American city not always noted for its friendliness to Britain, the Hood and her squadron never received.

*

While the speeches went on at the official banquet ashore, and while the mechanical pianos rattled away in the dance halls and dives along the waterfront, the great ship lay starkly beautiful at anchor, her searchlights probing the night sky of the Pacific.

The *Panama Canal Record* devoted a special issue to the passage of the Hood and the Repulse through the canal. They were the two largest vessels ever to use the waterway and the problems of handling them, especially the Hood, were considerable. The Admiral later commented on the outstanding efficiency of the canal operators and workmen, in passing his ships through without any damage or noticeable difficulty.

It was the Hood's beam that was the main problem. The width of the lock chambers in those days was only 110 feet, and this gave a clearance of no more than two and a half feet on either side of the warship, while her underwater bulges added an extra difficulty in handling. Since the usable length of the locks was 1,000 feet, there was not much clearance, either, at her bows and stern—about 70 feet fore and aft.

"Hood's displacement at the time of her passage was 44,799 tons," commented the *Record*, with its American love of statistics, "which means that at 50 cents a ton her tolls amounted to 22,399.50 dollars"—"and that's not hay," it implied!

So the squadron left the long deep-sleeper's breathing of the Pacific behind them and came out, for the first time in nearly a year, into the Atlantic. While the Repulse and most of the cruisers were detached to visit the ports of South America, Hood cut across the warm Caribbean to Jamaica. Trade-wind clouds lifted over the green island, and the jazzing and the drumming and the singing sounded out from the waterfront bars. Port Royal, once the chief haunt of the buccaneers, welcomed the world's largest warship with rum poured over crushed ice, fresh limes and tropical fruits, fried flying fish, and the local delicacy, spiced land crab. In the town where the ex-buccaneer, Sir Henry

Morgan, had once ruled as first lieutenant governor of the island, some of the sailors might have echoed John Masefield's words:

> Oh some are fond of red wine and some are fond of white,
> And some are all for dancing in the pale moonlight:
> But rum alone's the tipple and the heart's delight
> Of the old bold mate of Henry Morgan. . . .

Halifax was the Hood's next port of call, and it was here that the only political storm of the whole cruise blew up. At that time, there was a large section of opinion in the Dominion which held that Canada should emulate the policy of the United States, and avoid all overseas entanglements. The idea that Canada should contribute to imperial defense was scorned. A country, most of whose people lived hundreds of miles from any coast line, was unlikely to be interested in naval expenditure. Unlike the Australians, who were well aware that their underpopulated land with its long coast line must be a temptation to their Asiatic neighbors, Canadians felt themselves securely entrenched behind the bastion of the Atlantic.

It was inevitable that journalists should question Admiral Field on his views about Canadian participation in naval defense. It was equally inevitable that however carefully he phrased his reply, there would be some who were likely to distort his words. The presence of the Australian cruiser Adelaide also rubbed salt into the wounds of those Canadians who felt that their country was doing little or nothing toward her defense. Several papers pointed gloomily to the fact that, while the Australians possessed a fine trained ship considered worthy to escort the "Mighty Hood" on her world cruise, the Canadian cruiser Aurora (presented by Britain to the country after the war) was then lying behind an island in Bedford Basin "dismantled and ready for the scrap heap."

The explosion came when the Admiral in a speech did no more than tactfully suggest that Canada must remember that she had a long seaboard. When questioned as to what defense he thought such a seaboard required, he suggested that two cruisers at any rate would not be excessive. His answer was carefully framed, as if in reply to a theoretical question, but it was quickly picked upon by the Isolationists. "Admiral Field tells Canada what to do. . . ." The British Labour press and Party, ever eager in those days to find some way of discrediting the services, were quick to join in the fray.

"We cannot recall," said the *Daily Herald*, "a previous experience where the commanding officer of a squadron has been permitted to flaunt his personal opinions in public on matters of state policy. Are we to understand they are the views of the Board of Admiralty, and that he has been acting under instructions?"

Labour in Britain was still fulminating long after the storm had blown over in Canada. The Admiral had pointed out that several papers had misquoted him and they had printed his correction. He had, they agreed, done no more than give a straight answer to a theoretical question on naval defense. His tact, combined with the favorable impression made by the ships and their companies on Halifax and Quebec, quickly turned the tide.

"But for ships like the Hood, and the men who man her, Canada today would probably be German-occupied. . . ." commented one editorial.

The squadron's bows were now turned eastward. Topsail Bay in Newfoundland welcomed them, and then they headed out through the cold Labrador Current (the air like ice and the sea breaking gray and sad over the Great Banks) toward home.

The world cruise was over, the most successful exercise in imperial relations in the history of the Empire was completed. Millions of people in many lands had seen them. They had strengthened friendships and revived alliances. They had become a fireside story, and one ship—her photograph in thousands of homes—had become a legend.

II

The Spanish War

From the day she is first commissioned, until the moment when she finally pays off out of naval service, a warship never sleeps. Sometimes, if she is in dockyard hands with perhaps only a care-and-maintenance party aboard her, the rhythm of her life dies down. It never stops entirely. That is why a ship once launched and commissioned has a life of her own, a life dependent on the men who serve in her, but never on the particular individuals.

Even in the dead of night, in the small hours perhaps, when she swings apparently idle at a buoy in Scapa Flow or at anchor in Portland Harbor, there is activity aboard her. Men are watching pumps and gauges, minding fans and dynamos, checking oil and water pressures, or pacing the deck by her gangway to watch how she swings to the tide. Just as with men, so there are many ways in which a ship may die. Some grow crotchety and senile, and end in the breaker's yard; others die in accidents; and others through acts of God, typhoons or hurricanes that overwhelm them. To die in action is a noble end for a warship.

On the completion of the world cruise Hood rejoined the Home Fleet and in 1925 visited Lisbon for the four hundredth anniversary of the great navigator Vasco da Gama. Britain's oldest allies thronged the Tagus and the village of Cascais at its mouth to see this legendary ship—the ship that had traversed the ocean passages of the world along the route where their own great seaman (in a cranky little boat that could have sat on Hood's quarterdeck) had sailed four hundred years ago.

For two years she was with the Home Fleet, years of routine training, gunnery exercises, and local cruises round the British Isles. Now, for the first time, the Hood became as well known in her own country as she had long been abroad. Ports and seaside towns, estuaries and firths, grew to know the long gray hull and the mounting lines of guns. They watched the booms for her boats swing out from the sides as if by clockwork, the scrubbed gangways descend, the pinnaces and launches cut their clean furrows through the waters, and the sailors come ashore in their "tiddley" suits. Sometimes they heard in village or coastal town the deep rumble of her guns far out at sea—like summer thunder echoing round the hills. Sometimes fishermen and coasters saw the sky patterned by the white bursts of anti-aircraft fire as her crews exercised the 4-inch guns.

In 1927 she went into dockyard hands for a refit and general survey, recommissioning the following year under the flag of Admiral Sir Frederick Dryer as flagship of the Battle Cruiser Squadron, Home Fleet. During 1930, while the pattern on the Continent began to shape itself slowly toward the next war, she had her first major refit and overhaul. Paying off into Dockyard Control in Portsmouth, the giant hull for the first time since she had been launched was given a complete overhaul. Alterations were made to her gear and fighting equipment. The boats which had been sited between the second and third battery of the secondary armament were removed, and multiple pom-poms installed in their place. The pom-pom, a quick-firing antiaircraft gun with .5-inch explosive shells, was the Navy's first major contribution to antiaircraft defense. The guns had a resonant cheerful pattern in their sound and (for those were the days of Al Capone and the mobsters) were nicknamed by the sailors

"Chicago pianos." Water-jacketed and belt-fed, they were sound and practical, and proved their worth in many ships during World War II.

In 1932 the white sweep of Carlisle Bay in Barbados saw the Hood stand in out of the sea with the Repulse astern of her, and the cruisers Delhi, Norfolk, and Dorsetshire forming her escort.

It was January 21 when she dropped anchor and turned to swing to the long Atlantic roll and the steady pressure of the northeast trade winds. Viewed from the Yacht Club after dark, she looked like a distant city floating above the warm waters of the bay. The sound of the bosun's call echoed strangely against the piping of the tree frogs and the myriad noises of the tropic night. By day the ship's boats crisscrossed the brilliant sea, taking visitors to the ship, or landing officers and libertymen. Sailors new to the tropics felt for the first time the warm-silk touch of the Caribbean. Diving from the reefs they saw the convolutions of the brain coral, and the confetti colors of the tropical fish spinning through a sea that was still bright and clear thirty feet down.

Libertymen wandered down Main Street, Bridgetown, and found cool bars where the light-colored Barbados rum had none of the heaviness of the Jamaican, and was almost scentless. Old sailors lingered by the Carenage, the small-boat harbor, and watched the island schooners unloading or making ready for sea. In the still water were mirrored the antique shapes of sailing vessels that had been built at the turn of the century. The colored Barbados water police wore the naval uniform that was a legacy from Nelson's day, with the flat straw hats which had gone out of service use not so long ago.

Life was pleasant. There were cricket matches, tennis parties, and visits to sugar cane plantations. There were dances in private houses, in the big hotel, and in a dozen and one small cabaret bars in Bridgetown, or along the dusty road that leads out of town toward the Aquatic Club. The Hollywood bar was new in those days, its fresh white paint on the boarded front just beginning to blister under the sun. The shore patrol would look in once or twice in the course of an evening for, although the bar was "in bounds," it was one of the noisier and more riotous. Forty or fifty sailors might be in there, the old-timers sitting at tables drinking their beer, the young ones dancing with girls whose skins were every shade from dark ebony to sunny apricot.

A sailor had taken over the piano and the local pianist was listening to him, picking up some of the tunes that were then popular in London. Later he would reset them skillfully and lend them some of the sultry, spicy rhythm of the Caribbean. He learned the *matelots'* songs, some of them traditional shanties and others old music hall songs. "The Old Clockmaker" was one which I was to hear years later in that same street and that same bar. There was also a song which had been sung in Portsmouth when all the ships that anchored there were square-rigged:

> As I was a-walking down Queen Street—my eye!
> A pretty young maiden I chanced for to spy,
> Singing "Fol de rol Rio—Roll me down Rio—
> Oh roll me down Rio, aye aye!"
> I ran alongside her and took her in tow
> And yardarm to yardarm away we did go—

But at that point the song veers swiftly away into bawdiness.

The noonday surf was bursting white on the outer reef and the fluffy trade-wind clouds were grazing overhead when the Hood shortened her cable. A flag hoist to her main yard told the other ships to comply with her movements and get under way. As she slid out to sea the Repulse and the cruisers took up station on the flagship. They turned westward for the island of St. Vincent. From there they ran south to lovely Grenada, shining under the sun, and the Grenadines pearled across the sea in their necklace of foam-fringed coral. Port of Spain, Trinidad, lay at the end of their West Indian cruise.

Peacetime cruises fulfilled several functions, not least of which was binding together the peoples of a widely scattered Empire into a secure knowledge that their interests were protected. Foreign cruises also enabled the ship's officers and men to practice working and fighting the ship under varying conditions. They learned now what it was like to close up in the gun turrets, the director, and the control and transmitting stations in tropical heat. They learned how to handle boats through surf, or land parties of marines on unfamiliar beaches and coast lines. Out of the thousands of officers and men who were taught the seaman's trade in the Hood during those years, many would serve in other ships during World War II. Some would be captains in command, some petty officers, and others old three-badge sailors teaching a young generation of landsmen how to live and fight in ships.

The body of trained men which such a ship gave as a legacy to the nation was well worth the £274,000 a year of her upkeep.* If the Hood had been scrapped before the next war broke out she would still have paid her way. A tradition of seamanship is easily lost, and in a century when most men lived in big cities and towns, the old links which had bound Englishmen to their sea and coast line were already in danger of breaking. It was well that from 1920 to 1939 a body of men passed through the life of this great ship to preserve the traditions of sea knowledge.

"You will never enjoy the world aright," wrote Thomas Traherne, "till the Sea itself floweth in your veins, till you are clothed with the heavens, and crowned with the stars." Most sailors would be embarrassed to put it in such sonorous terms, but sometimes, on a tropical night when the watches had changed over and there was time to idle for a moment before turning in, they felt something of this. A big ship, humming quietly with life as she slides through a dark sound between two islands, and the wake is bursting astern in flowery bombs of phosphorescence, has a beauty that even the most insensitive cannot ignore.

Meanwhile in the shipyards of Genoa the new Italian Navy

*In 1934. Later the cost rose to about £400,000.

was fast building. In Germany the foundations of a small balanced fleet were already being laid. Designs for "pocket" battleships were secretly being considered and contracts were being placed for the construction of U-boats. The London Naval Conference of 1930 had reduced the defenses of the Empire to their lowest level ever, and in 1935 the Anglo-German Naval Treaty, by permitting Germany to rebuild her Navy, already suggested to the clear-sighted that, before many years were out, the balance of naval power in Europe would be greatly altered. The treaty allowed the Germans a surface fleet up to 35 per cent of the British. Later agreements were to permit the Germans to extend their U-boat building. Ultimately they would be building up to parity with the British submarine fleet.

The trial of Nazi and Fascist arms which came with the Spanish Civil War brought the Hood new duties. It was against this gloomy background that the Navy was committed to the difficult policy of nonintervention.

What nonintervention meant was that Britain recognized neither side as being right but hovered, helplessly and hopelessly, at the ringside. It would have been more reasonable, as Mr. Winston Churchill stated at the time, to recognize the belligerency of both sides as we had done in the American Civil War. As it was, our policy of nonintervention meant that the dice were heavily loaded against the legitimate government of Spain. Only the troops of Franco and the armed forces of Italy and Germany profited by our inability to see further ahead than the immediate problem. But one should remember that there were many voices in those days which whispered that the Italian fleet had the Mediterranean "in its pocket," and that the Army of Italy was as formidable as her Air Force, and—in conclusion—that we had better do nothing rather than make things worse.

On April 12, 1937, Mr. Anthony Eden, speaking in Liverpool, said:

"His Majesty's Government have had two main objects before them: first, to prevent the conflict spreading beyond the frontier of Spain; secondly, to preserve, whatever the final outcome of the conflict, her political independence and territorial integrity. In the furtherance of these ends we have from the first supported the policy of nonintervention."

The Navy's role in this was a difficult one. Primarily, our ships were there to protect British merchant shipping, and to see that it was not interfered with on the high seas. But the problem became acute as the bombing of neutral ships by the insurgent forces became a regular occurrence.

"The protests of the British ambassador," wrote Claude G. Bowers, the former U.S. Ambassador to Spain,* "were answered, after a long silence, with insulting phrasing. When this bombing or detention of British ships became a favorite outdoor sport without disturbing the complacency of the Chamberlain Government, the Labour and Liberal Parties in the Commons drove the Ministry into a corner in a five-day debate and they forced the promise from the Government to protect British commerce on the high seas."

The Hood, flying the flag of Admiral Sir Geoffrey Blake, was sailed from Gibraltar to assist in protecting British shipping on the northern coast of Spain. It was in April that the Thorpehall incident occurred. The British merchant ship Thorpehall had been stopped at sea on her way to Bilbao by the insurgent cruiser Almirante Cervera and the armed trawler Galerna. Hood, together with the county-class cruiser Shropshire, rendezvoused north of Bilbao in case they were needed. The incident was finally settled by the appearance of three British destroyers, at the sight of whom the Spanish warships withdrew. The whole situation was a difficult one, and infuriating for our sailors. Hamstrung by their politicians at home, they could do no more

**My Mission to Spain* (New York, Simon and Schuster, Inc., 1954).

than hover on the skyline, while day after day the merchant ships that they were supposed to protect were harassed and prevented from taking their legitimate cargoes into Bilbao.

The British destroyers were based at St.-Jean-de-Luz and it was here that the Hood now dropped anchor, her guns rendered impotent by the voices of politicians. When it had finally been decided that Britain must at least insure her merchant ships the freedom of the seas as far as the three-mile limit, three merchant ships left St.-Jean-de-Luz bound for Bilbao. G. L. Steer, who was an eyewitness, tells the story:*

> Hamsterley, MacGregor, and Stanbrook [British merchant ships] left St.-Jean-de-Luz in complete darkness before midnight on April 21; and at the same time H.M.S. Hood was seen to turn for the open sea, a constellation of lights that grew smaller and more spent until the horizon extinguished it.
>
> Morning broke with a mist lying off the Vizcayan coast, in the slipaway of the clouds from highlands above the sea. MacGregor led, Hamsterley and Stanbrook followed under her cover. But it cleared before they reached the sea at the mouth of Nervion. This time, Franco knew; his ironclads were there. The three British food ships were warned by the destroyer Firedrake when they were over ten miles off Punta de Galea. The Almirante Cervera and the trawler Galerna were waiting for them, the former well out at sea, but the little ship not far from the three-mile limit. And there, too, was Hood, the finest fighting craft in the world.
>
> MacGregor, still outside territorial waters, was ordered by Almirante Cervera to stop; she immediately sent out an S O S and the Firedrake summoned Hood. Vice-Admiral Blake asked the insurgent cruiser not to interfere with British shipping outside territorial waters. Cervera replied that her jurisdiction extended six miles off the coast.
>
> This was the final bluff of Franco in the Bilbao blockade. Having pretended that he had laid mines in Bilbao which he had not laid, and that he would resist the entry of British ships by force when he had not the force to do so, he brought out the old

**The Tree of Gernika* (London, Hodder and Stoughton, Ltd., 1938).

> Spanish claim, never accepted by Great Britain, that territorial waters extended to six miles from shore. And this bluff too was called; her eight 15-inch guns ready, Hood replied that she did not recognise the claim, and MacGregor received the message: "Proceed if you wish." She did. Cervera was silent. The Royal Navy's duty was done.

Their duty could have been done earlier, better and more efficiently if there had been more courage in Westminster. That, at any rate, is the story of how British food ships were enabled to relieve Bilbao—too late, as it turned out, to affect the final outcome of the Spanish Civil War, but at least not too late to prove that we were still able to preserve the ancient freedom of the high seas.

Throughout 1938 the Hood was engaged almost entirely in similar duties in the western Mediterranean. The Vice-Admiral had taken over the position of senior officer commanding the Western Basin. Marseilles, Barcelona, and Palma in Majorca came to know the Hood well as, engaged in one diplomatic errand after another, she cut through the summer sea. In two years' time she would be back again. But in two years' time she would be darkened, her bright work painted over, her crew at action stations, her wireless silent, and only the white sword of her wake at night to show where she headed eastward into Mussolini's *Mare Nostrum.*

12

The Guns of the Ship

A ship closed up for action is a far remove from her peacetime self. Now it is clear that the whole giant vessel is built for one purpose only—to serve her guns—the guns on which men, women, and children had skylarked in Sydney. The directors on which they had sat for their photographs, the control tower whence they had surveyed the milling visitors on the fo'c's'le, all these throw off any pretense at being friendly decorations. It is to serve them that the whole ship's company is dedicated. The gunnery officer who holds in his hand the firepower of this ship has an inkling of what it is like to be a god.

The first gunnery officers in the history of naval warfare were probably the "siphonists" of the seventh-century Byzantine fleet. The "siphonists" directed a stream of "sea fire"—a compound of sulfur, naphtha, and quicklime—through specially constructed siphons, wooden tubes cased with bronze. The idea was nearer to the modern flame-thrower than to the naval gun, but the defeat of the Saracens at Cyzicus is the first known occasion where such contrivances were used in naval warfare.

The problem of naval gunnery has remained basically the same throughout the centuries—how to hit one moving object from another. In a ship like the Hood, the gunnery officer had at his finger tips the control of four massive turrets and eight 15-inch guns, each firing a shell weighing nearly a ton. To bring these guns into operation a whole team of men, some in the turrets and some in the bowels of the ship, had to act with the instant reflexes of long training. To the inexperienced eye, the whirling activity inside a turret, or below in the magazine or shellroom, would have seemed as meaningless as a nest of ants when exposed to the light. Yet each of these apparently unrelated activities played its part in the grand design, which was to direct tons of high explosive on to a moving object ten or perhaps fifteen miles away.

In 1940 Hood was fitted with radar, or R.D.F. as it was then known, but, in the early stages of the war, range finding was still essentially dependent on the Barr and Stroud coincidence range finder. Each turret in the Hood, as well as the main control position, had its own range finder. The observations obtained from these instruments were fed into a central transmitting station which worked out the mean of the obtained ranges and passed it to the controlling officer. Innumerable corrections had to be applied to the ranges: wind conditions, air density, and the moving rate of range change during the projectiles' flight. In the transmitting station, machines were also busy working out the solution of the two basic triangles upon which all naval gunnery is based—one's own ship's course and speed, and the course, speed, and bearings of the target. The accurate solution of these triangles determines the accuracy of the gunfire.

A salient difference between the Hood and the battleships which were built after her was that she was a true turret ship. Her guns and the protection round them, which enclosed the working space, were all in one single structure. The whole vast steel edifice was turned by hydraulic pressure supplied by engines located deep down in the ship. In all later battleships, the turret, which comprised the casing over the guns, moved inside a solid barbette that was a nonmoving fixture. The revolving turret itself dates back to 1864, when the first examples were fitted in the old wooden battleship Royal Sovereign. During World War I a serious defect in British turret design had been uncovered by our losses at Jutland. This was the fact that if there were an explosion in the turret itself, the flash from the explosion could leap from one cordite charge to another all the way down to the magazine. Since the turret tops of the British battle cruisers were insufficiently armored there is little doubt that this was the cause for some of our battle cruiser losses. Hood incorporated the modifications which had been made to prevent this chain reaction. In effect, these modifications consisted of placing flash-tight scuttles between the magazine and the trunk up which the cordite charges were passed to the guns. The magazine was thus completely sealed off from the gunhouse above it.

"And they all fell to playing the game of catch as catch can," runs the old nursery tale, "till the gunpowder ran out at the heels of their boots." The innumerable operations involved in bringing the great guns to the ready would have seemed almost as meaningless to the uninitiated. In fact, the complete evolution of hoisting up the charges and the shells, loading, ramming home, and reporting "Ready" took a good crew no more than a minute. First of all a shell grab, operated by hydraulic power, lifted the shell and ran it out to the turret trunk where a hoisting cage took it up to the waiting gun's crew. At the same time, the four cordite charges in their silk bags had been transferred from the magazine on to the hoist. As soon as the signal was received that the hoist was filled, the operator ran them up to the gun-loading cage. The second stage of the operation was for the turret number to bring the gun-loading cage up to the gun. All was now ready. In went the shell, driven home by its hydraulic rammer so that the driving band bit deep into the rifled tube, and then the cordite charges followed. The breech closed behind shell and charges with a sinister metallic shout. At this point the gunlayer, following the pointers which relayed the director's orders, laid the gun, and the word flashed over miles of cable, "Gun ready!"

It was to achieve this split-second timing that the guns' crews exercised day after day. They moved like parts of a single animal, all individual reactions subordinated to the one end. In a well-trained crew the operation had become so much a part of their lives that they could have carried it out, wounded, blinded, or in their sleep. An old naval story illustrates the point:

A gunner's mate was home on leave, his feet up in front of the kitchen range, relaxing in his easy chair. His wife, who had gone upstairs, discovered that the bedroom was on fire and ran down calling out to her husband "FIRE!" Without a second's hesitation the gunner's mate jumped to his feet and opened the oven door in front of him. Seizing the cat which was dozing on the hearthrug, he hurled it into the oven, threw in the loaf of bread that was on the table, slammed the oven door, and jumping to attention called out, "Number One Gun ready, sir!"

The gunnery officer had the whole of this complex trained "animal" in his hands. For him something like seventy men in each gun—and turret—crew carried out their tasks. For him the transmitting station worked out and dispatched its information. It was his hand which controlled the end product of all this work—the firing of the guns. Except at night, when British fighting practice was to fire eight-gun salvos (on the theory that under the limitations of dark, a wider spread of shot gave more hope of hitting), the guns were normally fired in four-gun salvos. The right-hand gun of each turret fired first, and then, as it came to rest after recoil, the left-hand gun would fire. In this way gun salvos could be practically continuous, each gun being alternately brought to the ready as its opposite number was fired.

No one who has ever heard the clanging of the electric bells for "Action stations" can forget that tremor down the spine, that extraordinary excitement (a compound of fear and anticipation) which raises the hairs on the back of one's neck. The vast echoing hull of the Hood was often to resound with that urgent brassy rattle, and with the sound of running feet that followed as every man made for his station. In the gun turrets the crew would muster, while the turret officer and the gunner's mate waited to hear the reports. Soon the voices would come up from below, "Shell-room crew correct," and, "Magazine crew correct."

The gunnery officer hears the four turrets reporting, and knows that his weapon is now at the ready. The order to load is given, the turret officer repeats it to the gunner's mate, and from far below, in the dark silence of the ship, they hear the thud as the cages with the shells and cordite are loaded and run up. The rammers plunge forward, the huge breech closes and turns. In front of the gunnery officer a light burns as soon as each gun is ready to fire. Monotonously the sight-setters repeat the ranges. The turrets are moving slightly all the time as the gunlayers follow their pointers, and the hydraulic pressure swings the 900-ton turrets, each with its two 100-ton guns. A small noise precedes the storm, the quick, inoffensive-sounding "ding! ding!" of the fire gong. Then the thunder speaks—the deep shout of four guns hurling four tons of metal and high explosive into the sky. Inside the turret there is a curious shudder and a brief vacuum, or emptiness in the air, as the guns give their lunge and run back. The left-hand gun has been loaded and fires a second later. Again that sudden shudder and the empty feeling in one's lungs. . . .

The guns themselves were the standard 15-inch of the period, nearly 20 yards long and each costing about £16,000. They were a far cry from those early "siphons" of the Byzantine fleet. The inner tube was rifled and surrounded by nearly 200 miles of wire wound round and round the tube. Over this were the steel outer jackets, shrunk on to the binding wire. Each gun had a life span of more than 300 full-charge firings, after which the rifling was spent and the gun had to be renewed.

The Hood's secondary armament remained the old-fashioned 5.5-inch guns, only good for low-angle firing against surface targets. They were somewhat obsolete, therefore, by 1939, when a capital ship's secondary armament needed to be dual-purpose, and capable of forming part of the ship's antiaircraft protection. Early in 1939 it had been proposed that the Hood should be taken in hand for a major refit to bring her up to date and eliminate her known weaknesses. Had this been done her story might have been a different one. Unfortunately, it was the old cry of "Too little and too late." It was not the Admiralty who were to blame for this but, in a sense, the whole policy of England during those interwar years.

The immediate postwar years, with their uncertainty as to the future of capital ships and the economic restrictions imposed by the Treasury, had prevented this expenditure of time and money on what some were prone to think was the dubious asset of a capital ship. As the years went by—and this was especially true after the Abyssinian crisis and the Spanish Civil War—it became almost impossible to withdraw the Navy's largest ship from active service for a long enough period to effect major alterations.

The reconstruction proposed in 1939 would have replaced her old-fashioned secondary armament with the modern twin 5.25-inch dual-purpose mounting. This would have been a major improvement from the point of view of antiaircraft defense. The 5.25-inch mounting was to prove its worth over and over again, in the Mediterranean, aboard the "Dido" class cruisers. Other changes and modifications would have included:

(1) The removal of the above-water torpedo tubes.
(2) Modifications to her underwater protection.
(3) Removal of the conning tower.
(4) Fitting an aircraft hangar.

(5) New machinery.
(6) A substantial increase in her horizontal and vertical protection.

Some of these major alterations would have resulted in the removal of about 4,000 tons of unnecessary weight (the conning tower would have taken a considerable amount off her top weight). Her tonnage would not have been greatly affected, for the increase of her horizontal and vertical protection would have added several thousand tons. It would have added it just where it was most needed, and would have increased the one and a half inches on the fo'c's'le deck, the 3 inches on the main, and the 2 inches on the lower deck. Her side armor would have been less affected. The Hood could have stood up as well as most ships to torpedo, mine, or shell fire directed against her sides. A 12-inch belt covered 562 feet of her length to a depth of 9½ feet and thinned off only at bows and stern to 5 inches and 6 inches respectively. Above this, a strake of 7-inch armor-plating ran up to the level of her upperdeck. All her side armor sloped outward from below. This greatly increased its initial resistance, since it was almost impossible for a shell to strike it other than obliquely.

Had it been possible for the Hood to have had this major refit, her value as a fighting machine would have been immeasurably improved. As it was, there could be no hope of putting her out of commission in 1939. All that could be done for her when war broke out was to increase her antiaircraft defenses, as well as add other supplementary equipment. One of the principal problems which had confronted her designer when her armor had been increased after Jutland was to provide against the "bending moment" in the hull. With the Hood's great length, and with the immense weight of the turrets set so far apart, the stresses and strains involved in the center of her spine were enormous. But, with the outbreak of war, little could be done to compensate for the additional weight of guns and equipment which were placed aboard her.

Twin 4-inch guns replaced the old single 4-inch antiaircraft guns, and close-range antiaircraft guns were installed wherever possible, principally abreast the conning tower and round the after-control station. She retained all her old fittings and equipment (such as her upperdeck torpedo tubes) and had to accept, as well, the many additions called for by war. The effect of this increase in top weight was soon remarked. She had always been wet aft, but now—in anything like a heavy sea—the ship became like a half-tide rock. Great waves swept the quarterdeck. In the first winter of the war, when on patrol in northern waters, waves even swept the long expanse of her boatdeck and damaged the picket and motor boats. She began to show signs of strain. Her displacement which had originally been 41,200 tons and 45,200 tons at deep load had risen alarmingly by 1940. At somewhat less than deep load she was then showing a displacement of 48,360 tons and 42,462 at normal load.

Germany meanwhile had started the war with a small but comparatively well-balanced fleet. It was a fleet which, though it lacked numerical superiority over the British, had one great and salient advantage—almost all of its ships were new. Furthermore, it did not suffer under the major disadvantage that had plagued the Royal Navy ever since the Washington Treaty: this was the extraordinary *mélange* of ships, some built pre- and some post-treaty. This conflicting range of design and construction resulted in endless headaches for dockyards, supply staffs, and for general maintenance and repair work. On paper, the Navy looked relatively unchallengeable, but a closer investigation showed ships of so many eras, types, and classes, that their handling—whether from the commissariat point of view or in battle—presented an eternal problem to our commanders.

By September 1939 the German fleet, although far smaller than Admiral Raeder would have liked, still presented something of a homogeneous structure. There were the two battle cruisers Scharnhorst and Gneisenau, both armed with nine 11-inch guns, as against Hood's eight 15-inch. At first glance this would seem a major inequality, but though these ships were new, both were capable of 31 knots, and both exceeded their published displacement by at least 6,000 tons. So much for those who trusted to naval treaties limiting armaments! Whereas the official figures showed the Scharnhorst and Gneisenau as 26,000 tons, they were in fact nearer 32,000, and their speed (believed to be 27 knots) was 4 knots more. The Germans also had two battleships nearing completion, the Tirpitz and the Bismarck. They had three pocket battleships, Deutschland, Scheer, and Graf Spee; and three heavy cruisers, Hipper, Prinz Eugen, and Bluecher. Apart from these major fleet units, there were five modern light cruisers, a number of heavy destroyers, and about sixty U-boats.

If Hitler and the German staff had more fully learned the lessons of World War I—that England could be defeated only by sea power—they would have paid more attention to Admiral Raeder's admirably conceived "Z" plan. This was a model for a small balanced fleet that could have been ready by 1944. Fortunately Hitler never conceived as a first concept that he would be involved so soon in a war against England, nor did the German Navy command as much attention in high-ranking circles as the Army. Admiral Raeder's plan would have called for six battleships, eight heavy cruisers, four aircraft carriers, sixteen or seventeen light cruisers, and over two hundred U-boats, before he would have been prepared to engage in a war against England. Fortunately, again, he was committed to war with little or no option. Even as it was, the small German fleet was highly efficient.

By the end of August 1939 all our ships were moving to their war stations, or had established themselves on their patrol lines. By early September our measures for blockading Germany had already gone into effect. While journalists still wrote, and the public talked, about the "phony war," our ships were at sea day and night, covering their assigned positions. On September 8 the Hood, with her old companion the Renown, left Scapa Flow for the patrol grounds between Iceland and the Faeroes. Their duty was as inconspicuous as that of the rest of the fleet. It fulfilled the major purpose of controlling the northern exits from the only sea out of which a German threat to our merchant shipping could develop.

Midnight on September 9—and she was a long way from Barbados, from the cheers in Sydney or San Francisco, and a long way, too, in time. She was cutting northward on one of those unknown, unreported missions which occupy 75 per cent of the Navy's hours at sea during a war. She carried now her full wartime complement, close to fifteen hundred men, and there was little room to spare below decks. The hammocks were slung in every available space and passageway, rolling darkly to the scend of the sea. The working parts of the guns were polished as always, but everything else aboard was dulled with paint.

Darkness closes round the ship, blackout curtains rigged at every turn and corner where her hidden human world leads out into the night. There are amateurs now in the crew, temporary sailors and temporary officers. She is going out into what someone had once dared to call "the German Ocean," and there is no sound except the dark voice of the water at her bows and stern and—if you had been close enough—the high, sucking drone of the fans feeding life into her.

On this patrol the clouds were low over the water, the visibility was down to a few hundred feet, and even in daytime the ships could see each other only through moving banks of rain and mist.

13

North Sea, 1939

During the first four months of the war the Hood's role was unspectacular. Like the other major units of the Home Fleet her principal object was the containment of the enemy, and the prevention of his battleships or heavy cruisers from escaping into the Atlantic and playing havoc among our convoys.

Throughout the autumn and winter of 1939, flying the flag of Vice-Admiral W. J. Whitworth, the Hood covered thousands of miles of sea and ocean without bringing the enemy to battle. Straining their eyes through the gray scud, her officers and men grew to know the North Sea and the North Atlantic in all their moods. The North Sea they knew best of all—dour, inhospitable, and cold, even in summer it has a sullen aspect. Shallow, with little more than fifty to sixty fathoms in most places, it shelves from north to south as it approaches the British Isles. Almost in the center it is crossed from east to west by the Dogger Bank.

It was here that the famous action of that name had taken place in World War I, when Admiral Beatty with the First and Second Battle Cruiser Squadrons had surprised Admiral Hipper. The German forces had been put to flight, losing one of their battle cruisers in the process, and having another seriously damaged. In places the Dogger is no more than six fathoms deep and, whenever the wind is strong, it is notorious for its short breaking seas. The water is so shallow the sea even breaks in surf, and the bottom deposits are stirred up.

Ever since the reign of Alfred the Great, it has been recognized as a cardinal point of British policy that whoever controls the North Sea controls the Thames and its approaches. Only the Dutch under Admiral de Ruyter, who broke the boom at Gillingham in the seventeenth century, have been able to challenge England successfully in these approaches to her capital.

On September 25, 1939, Admiral Forbes, Commander-in-Chief of the Home Fleet, learned that the submarine Spearfish was lying badly damaged in a position off Horn Reefs, that shoal shaped like a hand which points out from Denmark toward the Dogger Bank. Unable to dive, the submarine was in a position of acute danger. The Commander-in-Chief at once ordered the Second Cruiser Squadron with an escort of destroyers to proceed to sea and assist the submarine. Hood and Repulse were also sailed, in company with the Eighteenth Cruiser Squadron, to provide heavy cover should any German capital ships venture out to interfere with the rescue operations.

The operation took place successfully, and the submarine was safely escorted home across the North Sea. It was an operation that was remarkable for two things—the bombing of the Hood and of the Ark Royal. The heavy ships had been sighted early on by German flying boats, and the attack was carried out by twin-engined Heinkels. The Ark Royal, who was in company with the Nelson and Rodney, had the first of her many narrow escapes—an escape which the Germans refused to recognize. On September 27 Hamburg radio broadcast the first of those complacent claims that would later become a joke throughout the fleet: "Where is the Ark Royal? Britons, ask your Admiralty. . . ." It was curious that they should claim only the Ark.

The sky was patterned with antiaircraft bursts, those false

cumulus clouds that spell war and not the peace of an autumn day, when a heavy bomb actually struck the Hood. "You never hear the one that hits you," sailors would say. No, but you often saw it.

"As big as the kitchen sink coming down—and twice as dirty!"

"I thought our number was up that time."

The bomb caught the Hood a glancing blow on her quarter and fell harmlessly in the sea. It was a chance in a million, a few yards farther ahead and the damage might have been serious. For a brief moment it had looked as though the bomb was coming clean for the quarterdeck. It had missed, and the ship was unhurt, but something had been learned. Hood's antiaircraft fire was neither heavy enough, nor well enough directed to deter enemy bombing aircraft.

Now there followed long days at sea when they grew to know every movement of the ship: how she lay down while the long rollers crashed over the quarterdeck; how she lifted her razor bows to a head sea; and how at night the air on the upperdeck was unbelievably cool and fresh after the fug and smoke of the messdecks. Youths, who had been at home only a few months before, learned the old sailors' tricks: how to put out a cigarette between the finger and thumb before going on watch, and stow the butt in the cap lining for future use; how to tie a towel round their necks if they were lookouts in an exposed position, so that the spray never got down inside their jerseys; how to come straight out of a deep sleep, jump from their hammocks, and be running for action stations as if by instinct—before the dreams of the night had had time to slip away. They learned that there was nothing like a good cup of "ky" after a cold watch, that the first cigarette after four hours of abstention was better than twenty could have been at other times; and that there was nothing like "duff" to round off a dinner on a cold North Sea day.

There were many unsuccessful sorties. Typical was the search for the battle cruiser Gneisenau. On October 8 Coastal Command aircraft reported Gneisenau, together with the heavy cruiser Köln and a destroyer escort, steaming north out of the Skagerrak and headed into the North Sea. Admiral Forbes had received previous intelligence that the force was at sea. The Hood and Repulse were immediately dispatched to cover the northern approaches off Bergen, in case the enemy was endeavoring to break out through this route into the Atlantic. The German fleet movement was, in fact, only a ruse to try and draw the Home Fleet within striking range of the German bombers. While Vice-Admiral Whitworth and his ships were speeding at 27 knots toward their patrol ground the enemy, under cover of darkness, had reversed his tracks and returned to the safety of the Kattegat.

"Wonder where we're off to this time?"

"Sarf End or Blackpool would suit me."

The sea flickered by, the same cold broken waves, with the white wings of the gulls trailing astern over the bursting wake. They pounced and dived in bitter rivalry whenever any rubbish was emptied over the side.

"Oh the sea gulls they fly high—
Thank the Lord that cows don't fly. . . ."

"I 'eard the navigator saying we was off Norway to the officer of the watch. We might catch up with a German battle wagon."

"If we do, I 'ope to God your turret's shooting better than on the last practice."

They found nothing. The Hood came back to anchor in Loch Ewe on the west coast of Scotland. At any rate, there was mail waiting for them, and a cinema show in the evening.

She was out in the same waters once more at the close of October, acting as part of the covering force of an iron ore convoy sailing from Narvik for the Firth of Forth. With her were the Rodney and Nelson, old comrades, "chummy ships" whose crews envied the Hood her graceful lines, and whose navigators envied her ease in maneuvering. The "Washington ships" were awkward on the helm, with large ungainly turning circles. The Hood, vast though she was, had something of the dash and sweetness of handling that only a destroyer or a fast cruiser normally enjoys.

On that patrol their search for the enemy took them as far north as the Lofoten Islands west of Narvik. They steamed through the cold waters where the tail end of the Gulf Stream fades away, and where the seas have a long range and sweep, all the way from Bear Island and the Barents Sea. It was now clear that the wartime additions which had increased Hood's tonnage had done so at the expense of her sea-keeping abilities. The engineer officers, who had their time fully occupied in keeping machinery running that stood in dire need of overhaul, were also preoccupied with the vessel's increased displacement. When tons of water boomed over her quarterdeck and the stern sat down heavily (seeming as if it would never rise), the strain was making itself felt not only in the superstructure, but in the hull.

Below decks, work was never ending, for it was essential that the largest unit of the Home Fleet must be able to keep the seas. But the older a ship, the more the maintenance. The work involved in keeping her efficient as a fighting unit had risen in direct ratio to her age. In press reports of naval war, it is usually the executive officers and ratings who come in for the honor and glory. The engine-room artificers, stokers, and mechanics and the officers who maintain the ship's vast power plants are too often forgotten. There is less glamour in the heat of the boiler rooms and less obvious heroics in maintaining generators and turbines —day and night, watch on, watch off—in keeping the high insistent whine of her fans going, and the great shafts turning. These are the men who, deep below in the hot heart of the ship, have little room for hope if she is overwhelmed.

In November that year, the pocket battleship Graf Spee, which had been patrolling in the Indian Ocean, was ordered north to attack convoys and merchant ships in the Atlantic. The *Seekriegsleitung*, the German Naval Planning Staff, decided that this was an opportune moment for the battle cruisers Scharnhorst and Gneisenau to make a diversionary sortie. Flying the flag of Admiral Marschall in the Scharnhorst, they headed north out of the Skagerrak and were off Utsire Light on the west coast of Norway by the morning of November 22. The first information the Admiralty had of German heavy forces being at sea was when an enemy report was received from the armed merchant cruiser Rawalpindi that a German battle cruiser was in sight. The Rawalpindi was then about halfway between Iceland and the Faeroes. Outgunned, and with a speed of only 17 knots against the German's 30, the gallant old merchantman under the command of Captain E. C. Kennedy, R.N., fought bravely, her seven 6-inch guns pitted against the eighteen 11-inch which the two German ships brought to bear on her. She went down with her ensign flying. Only thirty-two men survived.

Meanwhile the Home Fleet had sailed to cover every potential route by which the German battleships might break out into the Atlantic. Admiral Marschall's orders, however, were only to provoke a diversion and to stir up the hornets' nest. Although sighted by the cruiser Newcastle, he managed to make his way north before doubling back on his tracks and regaining the shelter of the Jade estuary.

This operation is of interest because, for the first and only time in the war, the Hood came under the orders of a French naval officer. She was lying at Plymouth, when the general alarm came through, and sailed at once with Vice-Admiral Whitworth aboard, escorted by destroyers. Vice-Admiral Gensoul, meanwhile, had left Brest in the French battle cruiser Dunkerque with two destroyers and the cruisers Georges-Leygues and Montcalm. Gensoul was senior to Vice-Admiral Whitworth, and, when the two forces rendezvoused in mid-Channel, he took charge of the combined group. Their orders were to proceed to 60 degrees north, 20 degrees west—south of Iceland and west of the shoal known to generations of British seamen as "Bill Bailey's Bank." The Dunkerque was a modern battle cruiser forming part of the French *Force de Raid* based on Brest. Armed with 13-inch guns, she was smaller than the Hood, but had the typical battle cruiser's rakish appearance. It seemed strange to many of the sailors to be taking their orders from a French Admiral, and for the "Mighty Hood" to be forming up and keeping station on a smaller ship. It was the first combined Franco-British naval operation of the war. Unhappily, it was never to be repeated. But on November 25, 1939, as they swept in harmony and alliance up the west coast of Ireland, no man aboard either ship could have foreseen what bitter events the next six months would bring about. The Hood and the Dunkerque would meet again only in the tragedy of Oran.

On December 3 the Hood was back in Loch Ewe for refueling. The Loch at this time was being used by the Home Fleet while the defenses of Scapa Flow were being hastily strengthened. The torpedoing of the battleship Royal Oak, on October 14, had gone to show that these improvements were only too urgently needed. As barren and lonely as Scapa, the Loch had at least the aesthetic advantages of grand mountainous scenery. Most sailors would have willingly exchanged this for the fleshpots of Greenock, Portsmouth, or Plymouth, but the Highland air had an exhilarating tang to it. Even an anchor watch at night was less tedious than in the Flow. In that brisk northern air the stars had an incredible brilliance, and in the mornings when the sailors washed down the decks the mountains were sharp-etched against a pale sky. Across the North Minch, quite clear on a day of frost and sun, were "the lone shielings of the misty islands" and the shoulders of Lewis gray and gaunt above the horizon.

The first winter of the war had begun, and the Hood's need of a refit was borne out by the fact that her maximum speed was now 25 knots. But still she could not be spared. Admiral Forbes' flagship, the Nelson, had been damaged by a magnetic mine while entering Loch Ewe on December 4. Rodney had developed serious defects which, temporarily at any rate, put her out of commission. Until his fleet was reinforced by other warships brought back from abroad, the Hood was the only active capital ship Admiral Forbes had in the whole Home Fleet.

The first phase of her war had brought no major action, no great glamour of heroic deeds, yet every mile she had steamed had served its purpose. Throughout the implacable weather of the wintry North Sea and the North Atlantic Ocean she had kept her way. Her actions, like those of the other capital ships, had insured that the flow of convoys across the oceans of the world had continued without disruption. As she left the Clyde on December 13 to help provide the cover for the first Canadian troop convoy of the war, her sailors could boast that, when it came to "sea time," there were few ships anywhere in the world putting in so many hours as the Hood.

"She's oot there noo," as the old workman on the Clyde had said to me. There was little rest for her.

She was at sea again on the northern patrol on Christmas Day, with the wind coming up and lashing the rain and spray against her turrets. There was that feeling of ice in the air. The sailors drank their tots and commented wryly on relatives who were "fixed up somethin' lovely in a factory job" or "sitting on a gunsite two yards from his own doorstep." They had their Christmas dinner and listened to the ship's wireless. Those who were not on watch "got their heads down." The others strained their eyes through the sea fret or stamped their feet and swung their arms against the cold. Deep down below, while the men on the exposed positions shivered, there were others with sweat rags round their necks, and overalls that clung damply to their bodies. They moved in the heavy heat of her boiler rooms or, amid the sighing whine of machinery, carried out their routine jobs—keeping the ship at sea and keeping her poised for action.

14

Mers-el-Kebir

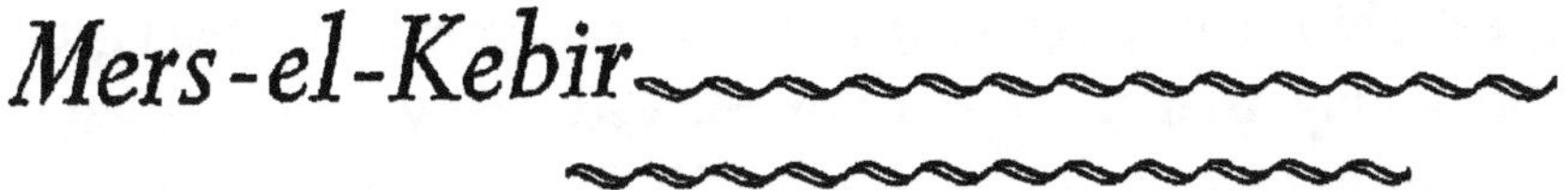

Ships and men were hard pressed in those early days. There was little or no relief from the long monotony of cold patrols, followed by brief spells in port for refueling and necessary maintenance. On January 1, 1940, the Hood was at sea again. She was back in Greenock for the second week of the month, and then out on a further patrol for the next nine days. All through February she was working from Greenock, and it was then that the long reaches of the Firth grew to know her. Salt and rust stained her once immaculate sides, and her anchor was scarcely down, or her lines ashore, before she was making ready to put out again. Her grace was still apparent though, as she swept up the Firth, fueled, waited for the mailboat, and headed out again into the early spring of the cold year.

On March 7, in company with the battleship Valiant, she returned to Scapa Flow. The defenses of the great northern base had been reorganized, but the work on them was still unfinished. It was natural that Winston Churchill, the First Lord, should wish to see for himself, and discuss with his service chiefs, the improvements that had been made to the Home Fleet's principal war base. He entered the Flow in a destroyer, followed shortly afterward by Admiral Forbes in the Rodney, with the battle cruisers Renown and Repulse in company. The sight of the great ships steaming slowly to anchor against the background of the lonely islands must have revived many of the First Lord's memories. As well as any man, he knew under what stress and strain the fleet was operating, and that the Renown, Repulse, and Valiant had all been laid down in 1916. Even the Rodney was thirteen years old, and the Hood celebrated her twentieth birthday in commission that year.

After a meeting in the flagship, where the state of the Flow's defenses was discussed, he visited the other ships. It was on March 9, 1940, that the architect of Britain's victory mounted the Hood's gangway. To the sailors, fallen in to greet their distinguished visitor, he was no more than the First Lord of the Admiralty. He was not yet the voice of their country, the man who in a few months' time would rally them in a desperate fight. Before the year was out, they would gather round the messdeck loudspeakers to listen in tense silence to that throaty voice, those pregnant pauses, and they would smile at those deliberate mispronunciations—the drawled words "the Na-a-a-zees."

The wind is ruffling their bell bottoms and lifting the edges of their collars as they stand there on a cold March day. The launch comes alongside. A bulky figure mounts to the head of the gangway, gold braid flashes, bosun's calls sound out, and the Admiral salutes. . . . A brief moment of history is suspended for a second like a fly in amber. "The First Lord came on board today."

At the end of March she was bound south for Plymouth, her crew happily writing those wartime letters which began: "Kill the pig and get some beer in the local. . . . I'll be coming on leave next week." Her long overdue refit had been arranged, and she would spend all of April and most of May in Devonport dockyard. At long last the engineer officer could get some of the defects erased from his defect list. The gunnery officer could note with pleasure that before she went to sea again, her eight 4-inch guns would have been increased to fourteen. There was no time for any major alterations and additions. She would still retain her secondary battery, her control top, and her upperdeck torpedo tubes.

Among the additional armament which would be added to her in Devonport was the U.P. equipment, or "naval wire barrage" as it was also known. U.P. stood for "unrotated projectile," and was one of the earliest examples of the use of rockets for anti-aircraft defense in naval warfare. The Hood was fitted with five U.P. equipments, sited on her upperdeck. Along with them went nearly ten tons of ammunition. This was stowed in thin steel lockers, mostly on her boatdeck, a practice which only the urgency of war could have made acceptable. The stowing of any form of ammunition in such an unprotected manner was completely contrary to normal Admiralty regulations. This U.P. ammunition was later to play an important part in her story. For the moment, it was merely something else which the harassed gunnery officer and his staff had to accept: one of the new "boffin devices" which the increasing menace of aerial attack was calling into being.

For nearly two months, while the spring tide of German success swept over Europe, the Hood was refitting. A contingent of her company, 250 men (mostly Royal Marines), were sent as part of the Allied Expeditionary Force to Norway. The ship herself was not ready for sea until May 26. Despite the restrictions of wartime, the blackout, and the shortage of beer which was already making itself felt, the sailors enjoyed themselves in Plymouth. Although the Cockneys, the Liverpudlians, and the Geordies might mock their Westcountry shipmates, derisively chanting the old rhyme:

"Westcountry born, Westcountry bred—
Strong in the arm, and weak in the head—"

they found the old city a fine place. Dance halls were still open, there were sailors' bars and restaurants, and red-cheeked girls. During the day those of the crew who were not on long leave were kept busy. The ship clanged and hissed with riveting and welding, and the clumping feet of "dockyard mateys" cheerfully disregarded the scrubbed corticene and teak, over which thousands of sailors in the past had spent long hours of labor. By night she was silent, with most of her crew ashore. She was alive only in a few places—where the gangway staff drank their cocoa and nattered together; or where an urgent all-night job kept specialist workmen busy, installing new cable or relaying another of the hundred miles of leads which formed the network of her nerves.

The evacuation from Dunkirk had begun by the time that the great ship put to sea again and headed north for Liverpool. It was a wet day in a gray world as she sliced through St. George's Channel and into the Irish Sea.

"Where we off to now, Stripey?"

"Flogging the same bit of ocean, I expect. You'd better get your warm clothing out of the scran bag."

"Wish we was down in the Med—taking the sun in jollay old Montay Carlo, what?"

In June that wish came true. The usual "buzzes" and "canteen" rumors had been circulating round the messdecks: they were to be based on Iceland; working from the Azores; going back to Devonport for a "proper refit this time"; sent to Singapore; or through the long rollers off the Cape to work from Durban. Now they were told—the Hood would rendezvous at sea with Ark Royal and would proceed to Gibraltar. There she would form the kernel of the new striking force that had just been called into being—Force H. The Admiralty had decided that our convoy routes between Sierra Leone and Gilbraltar should be covered by a powerful, independent force, which could also operate in the western basin of the Mediterranean when need arose. Force H would be under the flag of Vice-Admiral Sir James Somerville in the Hood. It was to be a detached squadron responsible direct to the Admiralty, and not coming under the orders of Admiral Sir Dudley North, the flag officer North Atlantic, whose base was also at Gibraltar.

On June 18 the Hood sailed for Gibraltar. The weather was fine as they ran through the Bay of Biscay. The long level panels of the Atlantic dovetailed into one another, as the swell lifted over the continental shelf. Shortly after 2 P.M. one afternoon they sighted the broad shoulders and swaggering flight-deck of the Ark Royal, wearing the flag of Vice-Admiral L. V. Wells, as she lifted out of the sea ahead. On June 23 the two ships secured in Gibraltar.

Hundreds of the Hood's sailors stepped for the first time in their lives on to an unfamiliar shore. But the Rock was never entirely foreign. The trailing lion's mane of the levanter cloud, the brassy shine of the sea toward Algeciras on a fine day, the machine-gun patter of the Spanish language—these might be unfamiliar, but not the atmosphere of the fortress town. Generations of English sailors and soldiers had left their imprint, so that the very feel of the streets and houses was English, and not Spanish. The beer might carry a different label, the sherry be a novelty, and the brandy sometimes a disastrous one, but the pubs and small cafés were not so different from the ones in Portsmouth or Devonport. On their walls old sepia photographs bore the memories of many ships, the Hood among them. The rattle of pianos at night from bars and honky-tonks brought back memories of Cardiff, Liverpool, and a dozen other home ports. There was always a singer among the company. A *matelot*, with the V of his jumper cut deeper than regulations allowed, and his flannel pulled down to expose the maximum of chest, would climb up with the band and give a song:

"That's my brother Silvest
Got a row of forty medals on his chest—

BIG CHEST!—
It'd take all the Army and the Navy
To put the wind up Silvest!"

Leave was given whenever possible, for it was clear there would be little rest for anyone in the near future. The Rock swarmed with refugees from France. Europe was collapsing like an old tree whose roots have rotted. While the sailors took their brief leisure at cricket matches and swimming parties, the ships that were to form Force H were being marshaled and the scope of their activities laid down.

On July 2, with the arrival of the battleship Valiant, the force was formally constituted and Vice-Admiral Somerville's flag hoisted in the Hood. The force consisted of the Hood, Ark Royal, Valiant, and Resolution, two light cruisers, the Arethusa and Enterprise, and an escort of destroyers.

A few days earlier, the Hood and Ark Royal had made a brief sortie with the aim of intercepting the French battleship Richelieu, and of trying to induce her to accompany them to Gibraltar. As it turned out, the Richelieu was met by the cruiser Dorsetshire and returned to Dakar.

The French were without hope in those days, many of their officers as well as ratings being reluctant to do anything that might compromise them or their families. The disposition and the unknown attitude of the French fleet and its senior officers was a nightmare for the British Government and Admiralty. Throughout the world, our naval resources were strained to breaking point, and here—in the shape of the unsecured French fleet—was an unknown quantity. There was the possibility that it might be seized and used against us in the Mediterranean and North Atlantic. There was an additional psychological factor which should not be forgotten in any attempt to estimate the decisions and actions of those days. This was the somewhat uncertain feeling which some French naval officers held toward the Royal Navy. Relations between French and British armies had always been maintained in terms acceptable to the Gallic sense of dignity and pride (a French general might privately consider his British opposite number something of a fox-hunting amateur). This was not so in naval relations. Unless one appreciates this factor, the action of Admiral Gensoul in the tragedy becomes somewhat incomprehensible.

"The Cabinet," writes Captain S. W. Roskill,* "was determined that there should be no hesitancy or weakness in handling the difficult question of the future of the French warships. Accordingly, early in July, the French ships which had come to British ports were boarded and seized. At Alexandria Admiral Cunningham's patient perseverence finally bore fruit, and Admiral Godfrey was persuaded, after prolonged and difficult negotiations, to immobilise his ships. Unhappily no such bloodless solution was achieved with Admiral Gensoul at Oran. Admiral Somerville was ordered to carry out at this port on the 3rd July an operation (called CATAPULT) designed either to place the French warships permanently beyond the enemy's reach, or to achieve their destruction."

It was on this difficult mission that Force H, together with eleven destroyers, was sailed at four o'clock on the afternoon of July 2. The Hood, Ark Royal, the two battleships and cruisers, together with their screen of destroyers, turned eastward in the Strait of Gibraltar and set course for Oran. The French naval port itself, Mers-el-Kebir, is a few miles to the west of Oran. Behind its harbor walls lay a powerful and potentially dangerous section of the French fleet. The flagship was the battleship Dunkerque, whom the crew of the Hood had last met on their allied expedition against the Scharnhorst and Gneisenau. Next to her lay the other battle cruiser, Strasbourg, the seaplane carrier Commandant Teste, two old battleships, Bretagne and Provence, and six destroyers.

In company with Force H was the destroyer Foxhound,

*Roskill, *The War at Sea*, Vol. 1.

carrying Captain C. S. Holland. He was charged with the delicate and difficult task of placing the Admiralty's demands before Admiral Gensoul in the Dunkerque. While Force H would remain just over the skyline, the Foxhound's orders were to enter Mers-el-Kebir in advance and transfer the British emissary to the French flagship. The instructions which Captain Holland carried were lucid and to the point. In view of the ultimate action at Oran, it is important to itemize the four choices which were put before the French Admiral.

(1) Put to sea, join our forces, and carry on the fight against the Axis powers.
(2) Sail with reduced crews to a British port.
(3) (If Admiral Gensoul felt that he could not break the Armistice terms and allow his ships to be used against the Germans and Italians)—Put to sea with reduced crews and sail to a French West Indian port (Port-de-France, Martinique, for example).
(4) Scuttle your ships within six hours.

Failing any of the above, the terms read, "I have the orders of His Majesty's Government to use whatever force may be necessary to prevent your ships from falling into German or Italian hands."

If none of these four alternatives should seem suitable to the French Admiral, there yet remained the option of demilitarizing the French ships in Mers-el-Kebir where they lay. This demilitarization (which must be completely to the satisfaction of Vice-Admiral Somerville) had to be carried out within six hours. It must leave the French fleet in such a condition that it would be unfit for active service for at least one year. To achieve this within six hours would have been almost impossible, short of exploding charges in many of the working parts of the ships. In view of the time limit, this last, or fifth, alternative was never a workable one.

Captain Holland arrived at 8 A.M. on July 3 in the harbor of Mers-el-Kebir. The French fleet was working a peacetime harbor routine: awnings were spread, and there was no steam on the main engines. The war was far away and somewhere else.

Meanwhile, at daybreak, Force H had lifted their towers and turrets over the horizon. From the Hood, Admiral Somerville signaled his former colleague, Admiral Gensoul:

"I am sending Captain Holland to confer with you. The Royal Navy hopes that the proposals made will allow the valiant and glorious French Navy to range itself on our side. In this case your ships will remain in your hands and no one need have any fear for the future. The British fleet is lying off Oran to welcome you."

Admiral Gensoul made no reply. More than that, he refused to meet Captain Holland. The British terms were accordingly handed to the French flag lieutenant, who returned with them to the Dunkerque. The time was now eight o'clock.

Captain Holland's feelings may easily be imagined. Entrusted with an extremely delicate negotiation, he was not even received, and was unable to assist in any explanation of the terms. All he could do was wait aboard the Foxhound and attempt to master his natural concern and apprehension. He had not long to wait. Less than an hour after he had seen the flag lieutenant report back to the Dunkerque, the French battle cruiser sprang to life. Awnings rapidly furled, clouds of smoke rising from the funnel and guns being cleared away all told their tale. The same activity was being repeated in the other units of the French fleet. Clearly Admiral Gensoul intended to try and sail—either to fight it out, or to escape.

What Captain Holland could not know was that the message which Admiral Gensoul had communicated to his own Admiralty totally ignored the first three proposals in the British document. He informed the French authorities merely that he had received an ultimatum: "Sink your ships in six hours or we will force you to do so." "To this," said he, "my reply has been: 'French ships will meet force with force.' "

It did not need the return of the French flag lieutenant to acquaint Captain Holland with the decision that Admiral Gensoul had taken. The gist of the French Admiral's reply was quickly given him. Under no conditions would the French allow their ships to fall into Axis hands, but neither would they respond to any of the British proposals. In the face of what Admiral Gensoul was determined to see as an ultimatum, he would have no solution but to prepare for action.

At sea in the ships of Force H, tension mounted as the time dragged by. They could see from the rising clouds of smoke that the French fleet was raising steam with all dispatch, and there were no signs that the French were in any way prepared to accept the terms. At 2:15 P.M., a quarter of an hour before the ultimatum was due to expire, the Dunkerque signaled the Hood that Admiral Gensoul was now prepared to see Captain Holland. It was, in fact, nearly two hours before Captain Holland was able to see the French Admiral. During that time our forces had laid mines across the harbor entrance, with a view to preventing the French ships from putting to sea.

As the minutes ticked by, the officers and men aboard the Hood waited tensely at their action stations. The period before an action is never pleasant. But waiting for such an unthinkable event as this, replaced the normal feeling of "butterflies in the stomach" with one of sickness and despair. Surely the French would accept one of the conditions? Immured behind their harbor walls, confronted with a heavy force at sea, could the French Admiral be so obstinate as to commit his forces to a hopeless one-sided struggle? Meanwhile, the range takers continued to watch the coincidence of the French mast and superstructures in their glasses, and to call out the range of their old allies. The turrets turned and the guns lifted.

Captain Holland was vainly trying to persuade Admiral

Gensoul to accept one or other of the conditions. His task was hopeless. It was during this uneasy waiting period that Admiral Somerville received a message from the Admiralty. It stated that a French signal had been intercepted, ordering all French ships within striking distance to close Oran and render assistance to Admiral Gensoul. Within a few hours, Admiral Somerville realized, Force H might find itself under submarine as well as surface attack. The Admiralty impressed upon him the necessity for reaching some solution quickly.

Accordingly, he signaled the Dunkerque that if one of the British propositions were not accepted, he would be forced to open fire by 5:30 P.M. The time set for the ultimatum had already been twice extended, but beyond this third limit the Admiral could not go. It must have been apparent by now that Admiral Gensoul was only playing for time. As the hours drew on, the greater was the likelihood of French reinforcements arriving. If the delay could only be maintained until nightfall, the French fleet would have a far better chance of escaping to sea.

Shortly before the deadline was reached, Captain Holland signaled Admiral Somerville with Admiral Gensoul's final statement: "[He says] Crews being reduced, and if threatened by the enemy would go to Martinique or U.S.A." This, as Captain Holland remarked, was "not quite our proposition." It was very far from it. What trust could we place, at that bitter moment of the war, in the terms of the French armistice with Germany? How easy it would have been for the Germans to deny the French sufficient fuel oil to take themselves to the West Indies, even if—and this we could not count on—the French sailors were prepared to follow their officers to another part of the world.

The ultimatum expired at 5:30 P.M. The British were reluctant to commence action. It was not until 5:55 P.M. that the most bitter and unhappy action in the Hood's history—perhaps in the history of the Royal Navy—was unwillingly begun. The brevity of the ship's log seems to convey all that need now to be said of that next tragic quarter of an hour.

1755. Opened fire at ships in Mers-el-Kebir Bay.
1758. Fire returned by French warships and land batteries.
1809. Engaged land forts.
1812. Ceased fire.

In those few minutes, while the hot African afternoon echoed with the thunder of the guns, Admiral Gensoul's fleet had been practically destroyed. The Bretagne, hit by a shell in one of her magazines, was a burning hulk. The Provence, badly on fire, had struggled to beach herself in shallow water. The Dunkerque, crippled and ablaze, had limped ahead to take the ground. The battle cruiser Strasbourg and five destroyers won their way clear of the inferno of Mers-el-Kebir, to gain the freedom of the high seas. Through the dense smoke, rising clouds of steam, and shambles of exploding ammunition and burning ships, the Strasbourg managed to make her escape. She was clear of the harbor before an aircraft from the Ark Royal spotted her. Despite a torpedo attack by six Swordfish aircraft, she and the destroyers escaped across the Mediterranean and made their way to Toulon.

It was an action of which no one could feel proud. In the final analysis, the escape of the Strasbourg and the five destroyers meant that it was not even a complete success. If the British forces had had their heart in it, it is possible that not even they would have escaped. The bitterness that the action naturally aroused among the French fleet meant that any likelihood of other units joining our forces was practically eliminated.

During the action the Hood was straddled several times, one officer and rating being wounded by shell splinters. There were no other casualties. Even the excitement of being under fire for the first time, and of hearing the screeching wind of heavy shells falling about them, could not efface the fact that it had been little more than slaughter.

Admiral Somerville had postponed the deadline until the last possible moment. Captain Holland had done all he could to convince Admiral Gensoul that whatever condition the French accepted would be rigidly adhered to. If Gensoul found that either of the first two proposals were unacceptable why, one wonders, was he not prepared to take his ships to the French West Indies?

In making any assessment one must remember the mood of that time, particularly as a French officer might feel it. Already German propaganda was cannily suggesting that Britain had deserted France in her hour of need, and that most of the French disasters might be laid at Britain's door. One can hardly fail to see how appealing to a Frenchman was that old scapegoat, *Perfide Albion.* An honorable man, Admiral Gensoul clearly had no intention of ever letting his ships be used by the Axis against his former allies. What he could not see was that, under the circumstances, Britain could not afford to leave large units of the French fleet in places where they might easily be seized by the Germans or Italians, and used against her. From the moment of his first refusal to see Captain Holland, until his last attempt to delay the ultimatum yet further, one is forced to conclude that the French Admiral had always intended to fight. It was illogical to do so, and he was in an impossible position to fight his ships efficiently. The fact remains, it would seem, that he could envisage no other way in which his own honor and that of his fleet could be maintained.

Night fell as the ships of Force H turned westward and headed back for Gibraltar. Behind them the flames still flickered over Mers-el-Kebir. There was silence in the messdecks that night, and a savage desire to "get at" the Germans and the Italians—the real enemy who had made this massacre of friends a tragic and unavoidable necessity.

15

Mediterranean, 1940

On July 8, 1940, Force H turned eastward again into the Mediterranean. To the south the headland of Ceuta shimmered with heat, while behind them the streets of the Rock were still cold from the night dew. A mist was lifting off the scrub on the heights, where the famous apes scuttled and scratched. There was a cool plash of hoses sluicing along the upperdecks as the hands scrubbed down their parts of ship, new-bread smells rising from the bakery, and the shrill of the bosun's call piping hands to breakfast. All the sounds and scents combined to give a strange illusion of peacetime.

> It was difficult to believe that there was really a war on. The Ark and the Resolution were in company. Everything peaceful as we steamed past the Spanish coast. Our escorting destroyers zigzagged on the flanks, and the whole thing looked like a fleet exercise in the thirties. So this was Mussolini's *Mare Nostrum!* It looked awfully like the same old Med to me. It was hard to believe that we weren't going to call in at Palma for a regatta, and then cruise up to Cannes and show the flag to the idle rich on the Riviera.
>
> . . . Lucky Spain! Their war was over. I could see the peaceful smoke from towns and villages lifting straight up in the still air. In the far distance the peaks of the Sierra Nevada were white

and shining. It was odd to think that our A.A. guns were manned, and that the destroyers were "pinging away" after real enemy submarines.

On July 7 Admiral Cunningham and the Mediterranean Fleet had sailed westward from Alexandria. Two convoys were leaving Malta carrying equipment for the fleet base at "Alex," and women and children who were being evacuated from the garrison island. East of Sicily the greater part of the Italian fleet was at sea. This innocent blue water, on which a light air was idly scribbling, harbored over a dozen enemy submarines between Gibraltar and the tawny Sicilian coast. Force H was headed for a point southeast of Majorca where the Ark Royal was to fly off her aircraft against the Italian base of Cagliari in southern Sardinia.

On a fine summer day the fleet steamed steadily into the Mediterranean. Night fell, soft and scented. From cape and headland the Spanish lighthouses stammered out their warnings. It was hot down below in the Hood. In the crowded messdecks the dark cocoons of hammocks brushed together. Sailors were even sleeping on the deck, their overalls rolled up and used as pillows under their heads. The humid dormitories were lit only by the glow of the safety lamps. At the head of one or two mess tables small groups of men, who had just come off watch, were sitting by the ship's-side lamps, over which they had draped dishcloths so that the light would not waken the sleepers. The tinkle of spoons in cups showed that a brew of "ky" was being made.

"Hurry up, Nobby! I want to get into my mick and catch up on some sleep."

Someone pushed forward a Benson & Hedges' cigarette tin containing homemade "ticklers." Several types of posh cigarettes were available in the canteen. They were mostly in demand when the ship was in harbor. *Matelots* going on a run ashore liked to take some "tailor-mades" with them. Afterward, the tins served as cigarette cases. All the sailors wore identity disks, swinging on thin lanyards round their necks. Some of them had small silver or gold identity tabs on bracelets round their wrists. They had bought these ashore in "Gib." They looked "tiddley" against a sunburnt wrist, but the old hands tended to scoff at them—"Kind of thing officers wear. What you want to waste a couple of quid on that for? If you gets drowned or blown up, they'll know who you was just as well without any of that nonsense."

There was a sudden movement near the entrance to the messdeck. Rounds! An officer, a petty officer, and a rating came in. They made their way, stooping, through the swaying hammocks, and went on into the passageway and the messdeck beyond.

"Yeah. All they'll do is put D.D. on your Service Certificate—and call it a day."

"D.D.?"

"Discharged Dead—that's what they puts down, chum."

There was no silence in the ship, even though the men making their "ky" would have said that the place was quiet as the grave. All the time the drafty murmur from the mouths of the fan trunkings sounded over their heads. Beneath their feet there was a steady purr from some piece of auxiliary machinery. The slop and scurry of the sea beat continuously against the armored walls of their home.

In the shaded glow of the charthouse the navigator laid off their course. The fleet was steering a little north of east. At first light on the tenth they should be in position, ready for the Ark to fly off her aircraft. There was just a chance that the rest of them might be detached to deal with heavy units of the Italian fleet. Down below, engineer officers in white overalls and engine-room artificers watched the machinery; stokers were busy over the valves to the oil sprayers that lit her giant boilers. The 144,000 h.p. that was being developed was enough power to light a town or to run its transport. Still, she was no longer as fast as she had been in her youth. Her full speed these days was quoted as 29.4 knots—and the Italians had two modern battleships just completed, each capable of 31 knots, and armed with nine 15-inch guns. Hood's total fuel consumption per hour was now 71.5 tons at full power, and it took a ton of fuel oil to drive her half a nautical mile. At her economical speed, though, she could still manage 13 knots for only 9 tons of fuel per hour.

Senior officers might spend sleepless nights, the Admiralty might be on tenterhooks, but "Jack" was not very worried about the odds that were stacked against him in the Mediterranean. They were tremendous. Italy possessed a powerful new fleet, and from her geographical position astride the central Mediterranean should have been able to dominate the whole sea. France and Algeria presented neutral but unfriendly shores. Spain, too, was neutral, but with a distinct bias toward the Axis regimes. The British had only three bases from which a fleet could operate, Alexandria, Gibraltar, and Malta, and each of them had its drawbacks. Malta could be rendered almost impotent by blockade and bombing; Alexandria did not have full facilities for dealing with a hard-pressed fleet; and Gibraltar was a long way from the main theater of the Mediterranean war. "Jack," with his conviction of an innate superiority to all foreigners, assumed that the Italians would be no match for him. But until Admiral Cunningham, in the battles off Calabria and Matapan, had proved that this was so, the Admiralty could not sleep half as easily at nights as the sailors in the Hood's messdecks.

Dawn on July 9. It was another perfect day. Night clouds were peeling off the face of the sea, and the decks were damp with dew. The first "Alarm to arms!" sounded in the afternoon, when an Italian Cant flying boat circled around the horizon and signaled the position of the British fleet. The air attack did not develop until close on teatime. For the first time the Hood came under accurate and heavy bombing. Later in the war, the Italian Air Force might become something of a joke—not to be compared with the *Luftwaffe's* Stuka squadrons—but the high-level attacks of those early days were carried out by the *Regia Aeronautica* with great skill and efficiency. At the eastern end of the Mediterranean, Admiral Cunningham's fleet had already come under air attack, and the cruiser Gloucester had been damaged by a direct hit on the bridge.

The bombers came over very high, in a tight formation. For the first time, many of the Hood's company heard the long-drawn-out scream as the fin-tailed bombs plunged downward—larger and larger until they seemed to occupy the watcher's whole sky. The sea burst into tall fountains. There was a rumbling crash of water falling back again; and the thunder as tons of sea raised by a near miss burst over her decks. With dull clangs, pieces of bomb casing sprang against her sides or scarred the steel turrets. But the Ark Royal was the main objective. Her great shining flat top was an invitation to the bomb aimer. There were moments when the Hood's company could not see their old friend for the great veils of spray that lifted and hid her.

The guns were thudding. The clear sky was patterned with the high bursts from the Ark's 5.25 mountings, and then at lower level from the 4-inch guns of the Hood and the destroyers. Most of the twin-engined Italian bombers were too high for our fighters to cope with, although one bomber from the second wave was shot down before it got within range of the fleet. Another was claimed by the fleet's gunfire.

"That's one of the bastards!"

They watched a silver-gray trail, with a glint of fire at the end where the aircraft's wings were bursting into flame—and then there was nothing but a pillar of vapor on the horizon, lifting for a second before the sea dowsed it.

Twenty past six. It would not be dark for some time yet.

"Here they come again!"

"Alarm to arms! Hostile aircraft bearing Red Three Oh. Opened fire at 1825."

How a ship shakes and thunders when all her antiaircraft guns are firing! The noise was tremendous: the pom-pom-pom of the "Chicago pianos"; the sharp rattle of the multiple machine guns;

and the bark of the 4-inch. Under the hot sun the sweat trickled down the sailors' bodies. They wore clean overalls with the trouser ends tucked into their socks, and antiflash gear covering their faces and hands. Before action of any kind every man was supposed to change into clean underwear, so that if he were hit there would be no dirty material driven into the wound. This precaution could not be taken against aircraft attacks, which might develop at any hour of the day, and in this respect were unlike a surface action, where the whole ship could strip preparatory to the fight.

There were two more high-level attacks before darkness brought its security. How one longed for sunset in those days! Men would watch the level sea and the declining sun, calculating whether there would be time for another raid before nightfall.

If the horizon was quite clear and the sea unruffled the old hands would say:

"Now you'll see it! Watch for the green flash."

Just as the sun's rim dipped, if you watched carefully enough, there was a brilliant green flash—or so they said. Was there really a flash, at that moment when the yellow disk fused with the blue sea? Or was it merely an optical illusion, caused by straining one's eyes into the flaming path of the sun?

"That's another day over. Now for the raid on Cagliari—"

But the raid was canceled, and Force H unwillingly reversed its course back to Gibraltar. The sailors could not know it at the time, but the object of their diversionary sortie had already been achieved. Both the convoys had been safely passed through on their way to Alexandria, and Admiral Cunningham, in the action off Calabria on July 9, had put the Italian Battle Fleet to flight. One hit (from a 15-inch shell fired by the veteran Warspite at a range of 26,000 yards) on the Italian Admiral's flagship had been enough to shake his nerve. As Admiral Cunningham later wrote: "[This] had a moral effect quite out of proportion to the damage."*

Curiously enough, the Italian Admiral, Riccardi, had been entertained by Admiral Cunningham in the Hood in 1938. Riccardi kept Southey's *Life of Nelson* on a table by his bedside, but, as Cunningham remarked, "His subsequent actions during the war showed that he had not greatly profited by his nightly reading."

The sortie of Force H was marred by the loss of the destroyer Escort, who was torpedoed shortly before entering Gibraltar and sank while under tow. There had been no damage from the *Regia Aeronautica*'s attacks. Despite the comparative accuracy of the high-level bombing, it was felt that the fleet had the measure of them. The Italians, for their part, claimed to have inflicted substantial damage to Force H. The Hood and the Ark Royal were both singled out for mention. ". . . In the course of the action in the area of the Balearic Islands, Italian aircraft caused heavy damage and set H.M.S. Hood on fire." A subsequent report claimed that the damage was so extensive that she would be returning to England for repair.

"I hear we're sunk."

"Not sunk, mate, crippled. We've got to go back to Blighty for a refit."

"I wish Musso was right."

There was only one thing right about the Italian communiqués, one sentence which, when pointed out, made the sailors laugh: ". . . night and day men are still working on the Hood. . . ."

They had nearly a fortnight in harbor: strange, still days when the boredom that is always just around the corner in wartime had to be exorcised by sport and recreation, as well as hard work and turret drills. Italian reconnaissance aircraft by day, and one

*Cunningham, *A Sailor's Odyssey*.

air raid by night, provided a reminder of war's reality. While the Hood's company were acquiring a deep Mediterranean tan, and drinking cool beer in the evenings ashore, they knew that back at home their families and friends were on the receiving end of Hitler's *Blitzkrieg*. When mail arrived they tore open their letters, their eyes quickly scanning the pages for any bad news that there might be, before they settled down to read them properly.

After one other unsuccessful sortie, this time out into the Bay of Biscay, Force H steamed eastward again to carry out the postponed attack on the Sardinian base. The main object of the expedition was to escort the aircraft carrier Argus to a position off Cape Bon, whence she could fly off twelve much-needed Hurricanes for the defense of Malta. At the same time, Admiral Cunningham with the Mediterranean Fleet sailed from Alexandria to divert the enemy's attention in the eastern Mediterranean. This operation, called HURRY, was designed to take place in two sections. The Hood, Ark Royal, Enterprise, and four destroyers were to part with the Argus and the rest of the force on the night of August 1, in order to carry out the raid on Cagliari.

The night was clear, the sea phosphorescent, and the sky brilliant with stars. While the Hood's crew watched and waited at their posts, the aircraft aboard the Ark revved up and took off to raid Mussolini's naval and air base. They watched the planes go with a feeling of admiration. Carrier-based aircraft strikes were still something of a novelty then, and the gunnery officer was forced to admit that for range and striking power the old "string bag" aircraft had the advantage over his silent 15-inch guns.

Their mission accomplished, Force H returned to Gibraltar. For the men in Hood, it had been another routine—and somewhat dull—expedition. In fact, not only had Cagliari been successfully bombed, but Admiral Somerville knew that his twelve

Hurricanes had been launched from the Argus, and had all reached Malta safely. It was an important operation, principally because it showed that R.A.F. aircraft like Hurricanes could be transported in aircraft carriers and flown in to the relief of Malta. This was the first time it had been done, and it established the pattern of many similar operations in the months to come.

Soon after they secured again beneath the Rock, there was a strong "buzz" on the messdecks—"We're going home! Back to Blighty!" For once the "buzz" was true.

Two days later they sailed, this time into the colder air, and the long ocean swell of the Atlantic. Admiral Somerville's flag was transferred to the Hood's old comrade in arms, Renown, who together with Ark Royal would now form the nucleus of a much-depleted Force H.

The Hood would not return to the Mediterranean. In her day she had traversed it from one end to the other. Both in peacetime and in war she had known the heavy dew that darkens the decks on a Mediterranean morning. She had felt the hot steamy weather when the sirocco blows across the sea from Africa, and the harsh days when the northeast gregale fetches the rollers with a thunder against Ricasoli light, and the swell lifts and booms in Grand Harbor. Her armored sides had grown too hot to touch beneath the sun of the midsummer Riviera, and St. Elmo's fires had burnt on her yardarms in the thick night of Mediterranean thunderstorms. Now she turned north toward the cold tidal waters of her native seas.

16

Watch in the North

By October the German Admiralty had successfully launched six raiders on to the all-important Atlantic trade routes. The enemy were now planning sorties on a larger scale, to be carried out by the heavy cruiser Admiral Hipper and the pocket battleship Admiral Scheer.

On October 27 the Admiral Scheer sailed from Brunsbuttel. She made her way north, past Bokn Fiord and Bergen, into the Norwegian Sea, and crossed the Arctic Circle to turn west for the Denmark Strait. Her voyage is of interest since the course she took, and the plan of her escape into the Atlantic, were the ones to be followed by the battleship Bismarck in May 1941.

The Scheer's movements were undetected by the Admiralty in London. She passed through the Denmark Strait on October 31, and the first news that she was "out" came on November 5 when she attacked a Halifax convoy. She had already sunk one solitary British merchant ship that same day. Unfortunately the ship, the Mopan, failed to send out a raider report, with the result that the Halifax convoy plodding homeward to England was unaware that there was a German raider at large.

The convoy's only escort was the armed merchant cruiser Jervis Bay. Once again it was proved that these lightly armored, under-gunned ships were no match for a warship. In the same way as Rawalpindi, who had been sunk by the Scharnhorst nearly twelve months earlier, the Jervis Bay was doomed from the moment that the gray fighting top of the German battleship lifted above the horizon. It was one of those tragic and noble actions—which star the pages of British naval history like brilliant footnotes to the main story.

While the convoy scattered in all directions, covering its flight with smoke and urging every available knot from the boilers of a heterogeneous fleet, the Jervis Bay turned and engaged the enemy. It was a fight against hopeless odds, but Captain E. S. F. Fegen had no hesitation. His action had the desired effect. It enabled all but five of the thirty-seven merchant ships to escape. For his self-sacrifice and courage he was awarded a posthumous Victoria Cross.

On receiving the Jervis Bay's raider report, the Admiralty immediately diverted all shipping. The Commander-in-Chief, Home Fleet, dispatched the Hood and Repulse, with three cruisers and six destroyers, to cover the approaches to the French Atlantic coast. It was the Hood's first major sweep for the enemy since she had returned to the Home Fleet on August 11. Throughout the intervening months she had been almost constantly on patrol, providing convoy cover, and working out of Scapa Flow and Rosyth.

The Mediterranean suntan acquired by her crew in Force H had long worn off. Only a parrot on the stokers' messdeck and a few souvenirs bought in Gibraltar remained as a token of the hot easy weather and the flying-fish seas. They had acquired once more the "Home Fleet look," and the duffel coats on their backs and the woolen gloves on their hands had come to seem like permanent fixtures. Time and again they had swept out into the northern approaches—west of Ireland, north of the Faeroes, or east of the Pentland Firth. They had found nothing; only the gray monotony of the sea, where wave opened upon wave like a yawn of ennui.

This sortie was to prove as fruitless as many others. Admiral Scheer was not making a brief excursion with a view to returning to Lorient or Brest, but was beginning an extended cruise deep into the Atlantic. Her presence there during the next few weeks was to cause serious disruption to our convoys. But to catch her in the vast area of the South Atlantic would have required many more ships than could possibly be spared. Our naval resources were strained to breaking point already, and the threat of a German invasion (even though it had greatly lessened with the approach of winter) still kept ships and men tied down.

So the Hood returned to Scapa Flow. Once again the routine was resumed—long patrols, and brief spells swinging to the cable in the lonely sound. The cliffs of Iceland knew her passing, and the cold waters of the Denmark Strait became her familiar sea.

On November 23 she was once more sliding up to guard that dark passage into the Atlantic. "Reykjanes," says the Admiralty pilot, "the southwestern extremity of Iceland, is a steep but not very high promontory, which ends in two points about one and one-half miles apart. Karl is a high, dark rock, about one mile north-northwestward of the southern point, separated from the coast by a narrow channel." At twelve minutes past eight on the evening of November 25, the Hood's navigator sighted Reykjanes' light and laid off a bearing on the chart. The dark rock he could not see, nor the rugged shore of the island, only the blink of the light, speaking out of the darkness.

Dawn next day found them in the cold twilight world of the ice edge which fringes the northern side of the Denmark Strait. "Determined limit of field ice in 67° 11′ N, 24° 37′ W," reads the log. Those long cold hours, watch upon watch of vigilance and readiness, go unrecorded and unpraised in histories of war. It is the brief moments of action which find their way into the sagas. But the reality of war is nine-tenths cold, lack of sleep, and eternal strain. Such patrols are unheroic, but they call for heroic virtues.

As the Hood's captain knew, the dangers of boredom had to be offset by constant drills and exercises, and by allowing as much leave as possible when in harbor; even if the harbor was only Scapa Flow. Most of his crew were "Hostilities Only"—the majority of them men new to the sea and ships. It was now that the trained backbone of regular officers and petty officers provided that stiffening of morale and discipline which made one unit out of fifteen hundred individual men.

Although large ships commonly received a higher proportion of the less reliable members of the fleet (the "skates" whom small ships had no time to train or discipline), the Hood was a happy ship. Few "warrants" were read, and the cells, or detention quarters, under her fo'c's'le were often empty. "It is lying in harbor that rots ships, and rots men," and it was probably the fact that she was so rarely idle in port which resulted in the contentment of her company. Not that all of them would not willingly have given a week's pay for a good run ashore in Sauchiehall Street, or "a Friday while" (a long weekend) in Devonport or Portsmouth.

She was at sea again during the second Christmas of the war, north of the Shetlands and east of the Faeroes, where the wind from the Arctic Circle steams over the sea like breath on a frosty day. At noon her navigator put down the ship's position, "63° 23′ N, 40° 16′ W." In company with her were the cruiser Edinburgh, and the destroyers Cossack, Echo, Electra, and Escapade.

By half past eight that night the thick fog (which rolls up so quickly in that sea) had shut down. It peeled away from the Hood's bridge and control top like heavy smoke. Moisture beaded the balaklavas and duffel coats of the lookouts. On the long, still barrels of the guns it lay like dew. In such weather, no U-boat would sight the ships unless it happened to pass within a few yards of them. The destroyers moved in from the flanks and took up station astern of Hood. The patrol carried on.

17

Battleship Bismarck

In the early months of 1941 the German forces had swept through Yugoslavia and Greece. Now they stood poised on the springboard of the Peloponnesus, and their eyes were turned toward Crete where British troops were regrouping after their evacuation from the Greek mainland. Everywhere the Germans still possessed the initiative. Belgium, Denmark, France, Holland, and Norway had fallen to their arms in 1940, and these conquered countries were now being consolidated as part of the Third Reich; their men conscripted as serf labor to work in Nazi factories, and their own factories turned over to the production of tools and arms to be used against Britain. The disaster, which generations of British soldiers and seamen had fought to prevent, had taken place: the whole coast line of Europe was in the hands of an enemy.

In the Mediterranean, the operations of the *Luftwaffe* and the U-boats were making the position of Malta, and of our fleet in its base at Alexandria, daily more precarious.

The only grain of comfort in that theater of war lay in the fact that Admiral Cunningham had proved decisively that the Italian fleet was no match for his own.

Our shipping losses were mounting gravely, and on March 6

a directive by the Minister of Defence commenced: "In view of various German statements we must assume that the Battle of the Atlantic has begun. . . ."

It was true that on March 11 presidential assent had been given to the Lend-Lease Bill, but the overwhelming problem of keeping our shipping life line intact still remained. Thousands of tons of damaged shipping lay congested in our ports and harbors, and air raids made the turn round of merchant ships increasingly slow. The U-boat campaign, backed up by Focke-Wulf air attacks, was being intensified.

The enemy's offensive against our shipping was greatly facilitated by the numerous bases which had now fallen into his hands. He had at the disposition of his surface and U-boat fleet the entire French and Norwegian coast lines, and his guns were being mounted along the French coast to increase the hazards of our Channel convoys. The threat of attack by enemy warships on our convoys kept a major portion of the Home Fleet tied down. After the attacks by the Scharnhorst, the Gneisenau, and the Hipper on our Atlantic convoys, the Admiralty had decided that, wherever possible, a battleship or at least a heavy cruiser escort must be provided. This meant a further weakening of the forces available to watch the northern passages by which German raiders might escape from, or return to, their home ports. The shortage of cruisers, which had been forced upon us by the Washington Treaty, was now most strongly felt.

The Commander-in-Chief, Admiral Sir John Tovey, had another grave problem to face. It was known that the battleship Bismarck and the heavy cruiser Prinz Eugen were now complete. In March they were running their acceptance trials, and from then on they had been working up in the secure waters of the Baltic. Fortunately, the two battle cruisers Scharnhorst and Gneisenau had been attacked by Bomber Command in Brest. The latter had been severely damaged, and in April the fast minelayer Abdiel had sown some three hundred mines in the approaches to the port, further restricting the battle cruisers' movements. The extent of the damage to the Gneisenau was not known at the time, however, and the Commander-in-Chief had always to bear in mind the possibility of either, or both, of these 11-inch-gun ships appearing in the Atlantic. But the threat of the Bismarck and the Prinz Eugen was Admiral Tovey's paramount concern.

The Bismarck and her sister ship the Tirpitz had been laid down at Wilhelmshaven in 1936. Although by the limits of the Washington Treaty they were supposed to conform to a maximum displacement of 35,000 tons, they actually displaced a minimum of 42,500. The Tirpitz did not complete and run her trials until June 1941, but the Bismarck was ready by the spring.

She was the largest and most powerful warship afloat. In 1941 she occupied that place in naval history which the Hood had held in 1920. But whereas the Hood's displacement at deep load, and even with her wartime additions, was at the most 48,000 tons, the Bismarck's was little less than 53,000. She mounted eight 15-inch guns as her main armament, and was thus equal to the Hood, but more heavily armed than Britain's new King George V class battleships. These mounted 14-inch guns on a displacement of 35,000 tons.

In addition to her eight 15-inch guns, the Bismarck carried a secondary armament of twelve 5.9-inch, and antiaircraft batteries of sixteen 4.1-inch guns. For additional antiaircraft protection she mounted sixty quick-firing light guns. She was thus more heavily armed than Britain's latest battleships, and larger and better protected than the Hood. In accordance with the ideas evolved by Admiral von Tirpitz in World War I, she had been designed as an "unsinkable gun platform." She was a honeycomb of watertight compartments.

In comparison with the 144,000 h.p. which had once made the Hood the greatest power plant afloat, the Bismarck had machinery of 165,000 h.p. This meant that although she was much more heavily armored than the British battle cruiser, she was just as fast. She had a maximum speed of over 30 knots, whereas the Hood, as we have seen, could develop only 29.4 knots by 1940. By 1939, power plants had improved so much that a battleship could achieve 30 knots without any loss in protective armor. The Bismarck was, in fact, a vindication of Winston Churchill's theory:

> If it is worth while to spend far more than the price of your best battleship upon a fast heavily gunned vessel, it is better at the same time to give it the heaviest armor as well. . . . The battle cruiser in other words, should be superseded by the fast battleship, i.e. fast strongest ship, in spite of her cost.

The Bismarck had the same advantages as the German warships built for the 1914-18 war. She was a fighting machine designed solely to operate on limited cruises. When she returned to her home port in Germany, her crew would leave the vessel and live ashore in barracks. The disadvantage shared by all British ships, from the Hood down to the smallest escort vessel, was that they had to be lived in for long periods in any part of the world. Consequently they had many more, and many larger, open areas—broadside messdecks, for example—which reduced their capacity to take punishment.

Like the Bismarck, the Prinz Eugen had been built with clear-sighted disregard for the conventions of the Washington Treaty. Laid down in 1937, she had completed her trials early in 1941 and had since been training and working up with the Bismarck in the Baltic. Although the treaty limits for cruisers were 10,000 tons standard, the Prinz Eugen displaced 14,500. She mounted a main armament of eight 8-inch, twelve 4.1-inch secondary batteries, and thirty-eight light antiaircraft guns. She carried twelve torpedo tubes, and had a maximum speed of 33 knots. She had a considerable advantage over a county-class cruiser. The Suffolk, for example, mounted the same main armament of eight

8-inch guns, a secondary armament of six 4-inch, but she displaced only 10,000 tons, and had a maximum speed of 31½ knots. The German heavy cruiser was not only faster, but her larger displacement was mainly accounted for by heavier armor plating. She was subdivided into more watertight compartments than any comparable British ship. At an economical cruising speed of 20 knots she had a 10,000-mile radius of action.

In April 1941 British, Allied, and neutral merchant shipping losses amounted to 687,901 tons. This was the highest monthly figure so far, and the situation was so grave that the War Cabinet had been debating whether it might not be better to cease publishing the monthly returns of tonnage sunk. In view of the general situation, it was little wonder that Admiral Tovey was deeply concerned at the probability of a raider foray being made by the Bismarck and Prinz Eugen.

On May 1 the Hood, with four destroyers, was in Hvalfiord. She had been based on Iceland to provide cover for our convoys passing to the south. With the increasing threat of a breakout by German heavy forces, it was clear to the Commander-in-Chief that a ship of the Hood's caliber was needed on station in the north. On April 19 there had been one alarm, when a false report had suggested that the Bismarck and an escorting force had put to sea, and were headed northwestward from Norway.

Hvalfiord is the name given to the long narrow inlet about ten miles north of Reykjavik in the southwest corner of Iceland. The fiord runs back in a northeasterly direction for close on twenty miles. It is only three miles wide at its mouth, and narrows gradually toward the head. Backed by barren mountains, the shores run down in waves of rough grassland to the thin strand. Except for the village of Innri-Holmur near the entrance, the fiord is almost uninhabited. At the head of Hvalfiord, mountain streams spring down the sides of the rough basalt rocks. In spring, when the snow is melting, these streams become roaring torrents, mudding the clear waters with sand and shale and topsoil. Although there are several rocks dangerous to navigation at the fiord's mouth, the fairway is mainly deep and the holding ground in most places is good. It was a useful anchorage, open only to the southwest, and a convenient place in which to maintain oil reserves for our ships on the northern patrols. The Hood's company grew to know this lonely inlet well in the weeks of April and May of that year.

Coming in from the long cold hours of patrol, they would recognize the bleak mountains that guarded the entrance, Akrafjall, a lonely table mountain on the northern hand, and the long craggy contours of Esja to the south. Sometimes the clouds would cover the stark peaks and intensify that feeling of being in some strange uninhabited land—a moon landscape where one would long for the sound of a human voice. On other days, when the sky was clear and pale, the fiord had its own strange beauty. Scattered farmhouses lifted thin smoke plumes among the foothills. In the still air at night the stars were crisp as brilliants.

In March the Hood had completed a refit, in the course of which she had been fitted with a new type of gunnery radar set —designed to supplement her optical range finders. The set would give accurate results on a large target like a battleship up to ten miles' distance. It was not a search radar set of the new type which was then being fitted to the King George V class battleships.

Immediately on completion of the refit, the Hood had gone to sea on Atlantic and northern patrols. There had been no time to work her up to high standards of efficiency. Changes in her ship's company and changes in her fighting equipment would, under normal conditions, have demanded a period of weeks, or even months, of intensive "work-up." There was no time for this in 1941. (In the easier situation of the 1914–18 war, Admiral Jellicoe would not accept a capital ship as a competent seagoing unit of the Grand Fleet until her company had spent two months attaining full fighting efficiency.) When a ship is almost constantly on patrol, coming in only for a quick turn round, just to refuel and put to sea again, there is almost no opportunity for exercising her crew in the precisions called for by modern gunnery. The Bismarck, in the peaceful Baltic, suffered from no such disadvantages.

The German Operation RHEINUEBUNG had originally been timed to take place at the end of April. It had been delayed for a little over a fortnight because the Prinz Eugen was damaged by a magnetic mine on April 23. The object of RHEINUEBUNG was for the Bismarck and Prinz Eugen to make their way via the Denmark Strait into the Atlantic. Since the other battleship Tirpitz was not yet ready, there was no question of attempting to destroy our battleship escorts along with their convoys. That, it was hoped, would come at a later date, when both Bismarck and Tirpitz would be operating in company. In the meantime, for this first sortie by the new German battleship, her role was to tie down our battleships in the Atlantic by the very fact of her presence there, while the Prinz Eugen was free to destroy the merchantmen. The German Admiralty was confident that the Bismarck would be a match for any single British battleship she might encounter. They were, of course, also aware that our resources were so strained that there was little or no likelihood of her encountering a convoy escorted by two or more battleships. To provoke anything in the nature of a fleet action was naturally to be avoided.

An operation of this type requires careful planning. Unlike the British fleet, the Germans were deprived of the use of any ports in America or Africa, although they now had the French Atlantic ports to put into should need arise. During the execution of RHEINUEBUNG they would be at sea for a lengthy period, the time of which would necessarily depend on what success they achieved, and whether or not they suffered any damage. To insure that if things went well they would be able to prolong their cruise, five oil tankers (the Belchen, Gedania, Gonzenheim, Esso-

Hamburg, and Friedrich Breme) were sailed in advance to take up their allotted stations. They would provide fueling points for the raiders over an area ranging from the coast of Greenland to the South Atlantic. Two supply ships carrying ammunition and victuals were also sailed to complete the "fleet train" for the Bismarck and Prinz Eugen. Vice-Admiral Lutjens, wearing his flag in the Bismarck, would be in command of the operation.

Lutjens was a naval officer who had already proved his ability in the Scharnhorst and Gneisenau sortie of January—March 1941. Admiral Raeder and the German Naval Staff had been well pleased with the success of that operation, in the course of which twenty-two merchant ships had been sunk. It was confidently expected that with the new battleship Bismarck under his command the Admiral would prove even more successful. Lutjens himself was not so sanguine about the prospects, particularly since it was now known that the two battle cruisers, Scharnhorst and Gneisenau, would not be able to make a diversionary raid out of Brest to help cover his movements. The delay caused by the damage to the Prinz Eugen weakened his case, for in the meantime the German attack on Crete had been prepared. On the morning of May 20 the German airborne troops would start their drop on the island. Now, if ever, seemed the moment when, with British resources strained to their limit, a large-scale foray into the Atlantic would pay dividends. RHEINUEBUNG did not envisage any special co-operation between the two German surface ships and their U-boats on patrol in the Atlantic.

On May 18 the Bismarck and Prinz Eugen sailed from Gdynia in Poland. They made their way along the quiet Baltic coast and turned north through the narrows between Denmark and Norway—occupied countries now, where German soldiers watched with pride these two great representatives of the Third Reich heading seaward into the Kattegat. Although every effort had been made to give the illusion that this was no more than a further exercise in the working-up program of the two ships, British

Intelligence was quickly on the alert. Early on the morning of May 21, at the moment when Admiral Lutjens' ships were dropping anchor in Kors Fiord near Bergen, intelligence reached Whitehall that two German heavy fleet units had been seen steaming northward through the Kattegat on the previous day. They were escorted, said the report, by a number of destroyers, and were accompanied by several merchant ships. Admiral Sir John Tovey, in his flagship, King George V, at Scapa Flow, was immediately acquainted with the news.

There are five potential routes which a ship bent on escaping from the North Sea into the North Atlantic may take. One of them, through the Pentland Firth between Scotland and the Orkneys, might immediately be dismissed, since this would bring the enemy directly under the guns of the Home Fleet in its base at Scapa Flow. The other four routes were all conceivable, but they increased in probability the farther away they were from our sea and air patrols. The second route was through the Fair Island channel between the Shetlands and the Orkneys. This again, because of its nearness to the British fleet base, was unlikely but could not be entirely ruled out—particularly if weather conditions should be heavy and visibility bad. The third way, between the Shetlands and the Faeroes, a channel of about 160 miles, was more likely. The widest channel was the fourth, between the Faeroes and the southeastern coast of Iceland, nearly 250 miles. The fifth was the most probable, even though it was the narrowest. This was through the Denmark Strait between Iceland and Greenland, where at this time of the year the Greenland ice pack would have left only about 60 miles of navigable sea. But weather conditions here were likely to be bad, and the efficiency of our sea and air patrols reduced accordingly.

The first problem which confronted the Commander-in-Chief was the question of the enemy's intentions. He had no definite information as yet that the Bismarck was one of the German warships reported on their way north. But he had many reasons for thinking that—having completed her Baltic training—she was probably ready for her first operation. The fact that the two German warships were reported as being in company with a number of merchantmen suggested that some troop movement was being made. For some weeks past there had been rumors that the enemy might be contemplating an invasion of the Faeroes or Iceland. This was an eventuality which the Admiral had to bear in mind. On the other hand, it seemed more likely that this was no more than a routine movement of cargo ships and transports to reinforce the Norway garrisons, designed perhaps to screen the real intentions of the warships. Since the British fleet held the command of the sea, an invasion of Iceland or the Faeroes (however successful in the first instance) could not achieve a permanent success. The greatest danger, at that moment in the war, would result from a breakout by German heavy units into the Atlantic. It was against this eventuality that Admiral Tovey made his dispositions.

The first necessity was to ascertain whether or not the two warships were at anchor in Norwegian waters. If they had already sailed, every minute became vital. While he waited for further news, all ships in Scapa Flow were brought to two hours' notice for steam. On May 21, a Spitfire on reconnaissance patrol sighted and photographed two warships lying in a fiord south of Bergen. The time was 1:15 P.M. The Bismarck was not immediately identified, and the Spitfire pilot's first estimation was that the ships were two cruisers. Examination of the photographs quickly corrected this mistake. The Bismarck and a heavy cruiser of the Hipper class were correctly identified.

On the afternoon of May 21, the weather shut down. Rain was sweeping the North Sea, and the outlook for any further air reconnaissance became increasingly bleak. The Commander-in-Chief was faced with an unenviable problem. He now knew the identity of the two ships, but he still could have no idea of their intentions. Bergen seemed an unlikely place for the Germans to be in if they were planning a breakout through the Denmark Strait. From such a position—almost opposite the Shetlands—it seemed that if an Atlantic breakout was contemplated, the enemy might be favoring one of the southern channels. All the same, the fact that they were in Bergen at all—which, as the Germans well knew, was within the range of our air patrols—suggested that the Bismarck and the cruiser had been doing no more than escort a convoy to Norway, and would shortly be returning to the Baltic. In any case, the Commander-in-Chief could not afford to ignore the threat implicit in their presence in northern waters. The county-class cruiser Norfolk was already on patrol in the Denmark Strait, while her sister ship the Suffolk was refueling in Hvalfiord. The latter was instructed to complete with fuel and be prepared to rejoin the Norfolk.

Throughout the afternoon of the twenty-first, weather conditions worsened. There was little chance of any further aerial reconnaissance to bring the Admiral news of the enemy's movements. The next day might bring improved conditions, but before then the Germans might make their escape. While he would hold back the main body of the Home Fleet—in case further information came through—the Commander-in-Chief decided that he must, at any rate, cover the northern approaches to the Atlantic with a force of heavy ships. It was no moment for himself to put to sea in his flagship, King George V. The instant that his telephone link from the buoy to the Admiralty was severed, his access to information would be severely limited by the necessities of wireless silence. The Prince of Wales and the Hood, however, were both at his disposal.

The Hood had recently returned from Hvalfiord and was now wearing the flag of Vice-Admiral L. E. Holland, C.B. Admiral Holland had relieved Vice-Admiral Whitworth on May 11 and had taken over Second-in-Command of the Home Fleet. In command of the Hood was Captain R. Kerr, who had taken over from Captain I. G. Glennie in 1940.

As night fell over the Orkneys, and no further news came through, Admiral Tovey decided to sail the Hood and the Prince of Wales. With them would go the six destroyers Achates, Antelope, Anthony, Echo, Electra, and Icarus. The force would make for Hvalfiord and refuel. They would hold themselves in readiness for any attempted breakout by the Bismarck and the heavy cruiser.

Midnight May 21, 1941. The clank of cable coming in was followed by a sighing hush as the ship's bows turned toward the sea and the north.

"What's the buzz?"

"Hovelford."

"Not again!"

So many times in her long career she had sailed from this ring of Viking islands. Now, as always, there accompanied her the sad cries of the molliemawks, and the song of the wind over the tangled hills. The islands were dark against the sky, and the boom gates were closing behind Admiral Holland's force.

> Be it wind, be it weet, be it hail, be it sleet,
> Our ship must sail the faem. . . .

18

Into the Arctic Circle

Two hours before Admiral Holland's ships sailed from Scapa Flow, the Bismarck had slipped out from Bergen and sailed for the north. Admiral Lutjens' ships were complete with fuel, and a feeling of optimism possessed the German sailors. They knew that British air reconnaissance had sighted them in their hideout, but they were not unduly worried. It was unlikely, they felt, that the British would expect them to make a dash for the Denmark Strait from a point so far to the south of Iceland. The weather was coming down thick, and there was a good chance that the British would be unable to get any further news of them during the next day, May 22. Nothing could have suited Admiral Lutjens better. With any luck, by the time that further reconnaissance planes had got over to discover the empty fiord, he and his two ships would be through the Denmark Strait—with all the immensity of the Atlantic in which to operate, and in which to hide.

The morning of the twenty-second broke gray and cheerless over the North Sea. The weather had further deteriorated, and the chances of flying off any air patrols grew steadily worse. Admiral Tovey's anxiety can well be imagined. It was over twelve hours since he had received any news of the enemy. If they had sailed overnight, they would now be well on their way. The temptation to put to sea himself must have been almost irresistible. Yet no one knew better than he that the overriding factor was the question of fuel oil. If he were to put out now—and if the German ships were still in harbor south of Bergen—he would merely be wasting precious fuel. If the Germans were then to make a breakout at a later date, he might find himself with all his ships in need of fuel, while the Bismarck and the cruiser with her would be topped up. The Germans had the initiative on their side. The British Commander-in-Chief, with an inadequate fleet, had four escape routes to cover, involving thousands of square miles.

Athough on paper the ships at Admiral Tovey's disposal seem to suggest an overwhelming preponderance, a number of factors must be taken into consideration. The Hood and the Prince of Wales were now well on their way toward Hvalfiord. There remained his own flagship, the King George V, and the veteran battle cruiser Repulse. The latter had been waiting in the Clyde to escort a convoy to Gibraltar, but had now been put at his disposal by the Admiralty. He had, therefore, two battleships and two battle cruisers with him to meet one battleship and one heavy cruiser. But he had first of all to find the enemy, and to find the enemy in full force was clearly impossible. The Admiralty had also put at his disposal the aircraft carrier Victorious, who had been waiting at Scapa Flow to embark aircraft for the same convoy duty as the Repulse.

Not least of the Admiral's problems was the state of his ships. The Hood and Repulse were old, and the Repulse mounted two less guns than the Bismarck. She was also insufficiently armored. The Prince of Wales, on the other hand, had joined the fleet only about seven weeks before, and was far from battleworthy. Her 14-inch turrets were of a new type, and numerous teething troubles had occurred in them. In fact, when she sailed with the Hood for Hvalfiord she still had a number of the contractor's workmen aboard. Only the urgent needs of those days could have justified sending a brand-new, and virtually untrained, ship out to meet a battleship of heavier caliber—a battleship known to have completed its training and to be in the first degree of efficiency.

The aircraft carrier Victorious was in a similar state to the Prince of Wales. She had commissioned only two months before and the Gibraltar convoy, from which she had now been diverted, would have been her first real operation. It would have been something in the nature of a shake-down cruise for her. Of the other ships at Sir John Tovey's disposal, the two cruisers Birmingham and Manchester were patrolling the Iceland–Faeroes channel. The cruiser Arethusa had just put into Reykjavik in Iceland, and was held there pending further news. The cruiser Hermione was on her way to join the Commander-in-Chief in Scapa Flow.

The cloud base was low over the North Sea, and still no news came through. On the afternoon of May 22 Captain H. St. J. Fancourt, R.N., in command of the Royal Naval Air Station at Hatston, which was on Mainland near Kirkwall, asked permission from Coastal Command and from Admiral Tovey to fly off a twin-engined Maryland bomber, on a reconnaissance flight to Bergen. All day, Captain Fancourt had been hoping to fly off a squadron of Albacore torpedo planes, in a strike against the German warships. These aircraft were normally based at Hatston, but he had moved them up to the Shetlands to increase their range. The fact that there was no air reconnaissance on account of the bad weather meant that no strike could be carried out, and so—aware that his Commander-in-Chief must be fretting for news of the enemy—he cast around for a suitable aircraft and crew to make the attempt to reach Bergen. He had a suitable aircraft available in a Maryland, which had long endurance and had been stripped of its operational equipment to make it suitable for target towing. As crew he found an experienced pilot in

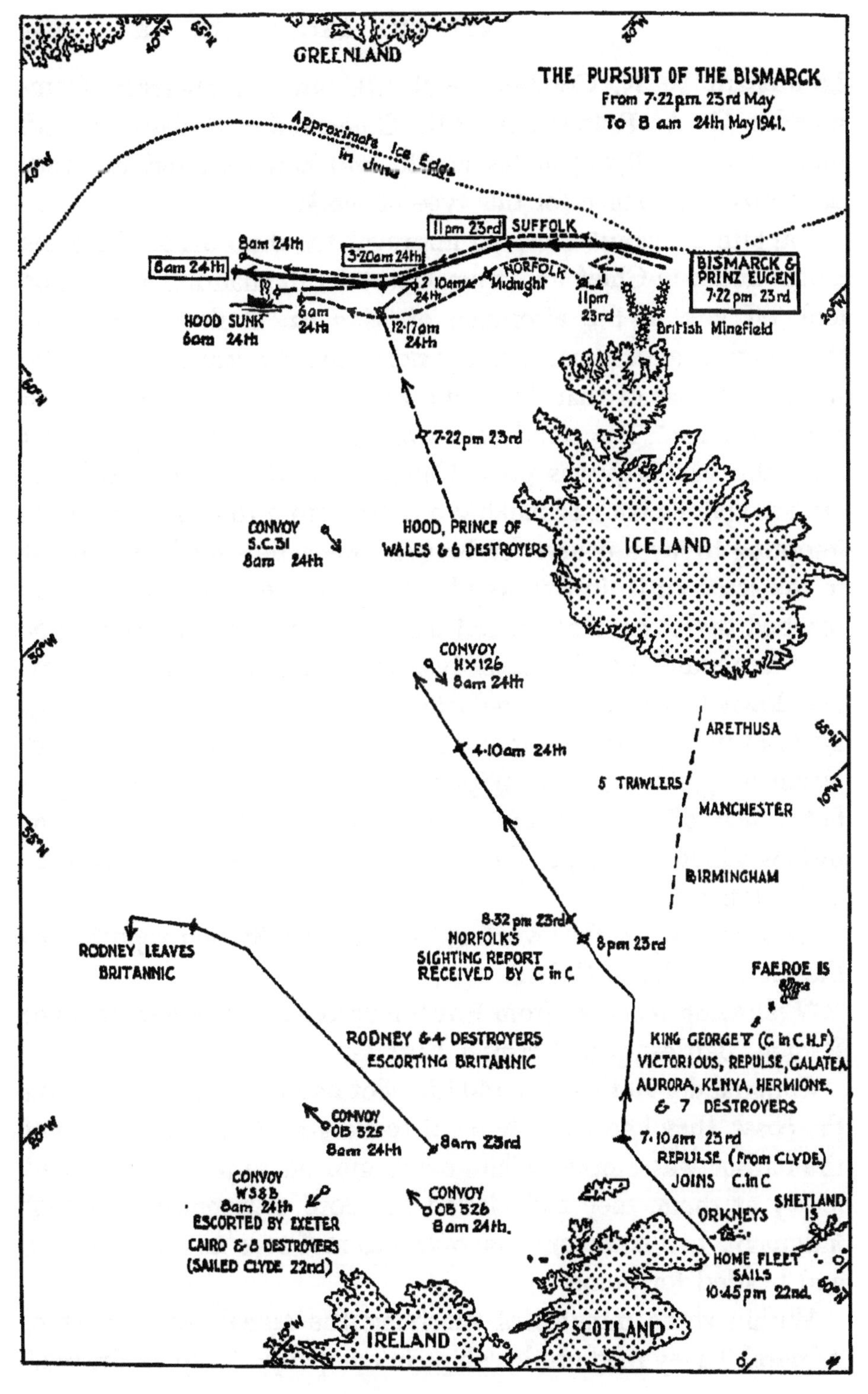
GREENLAND
THE PURSUIT OF THE BISMARCK
From 7·22 pm. 23rd May
To 8 am 24th May 1941.
Approximate Ice Edge in June
11pm 23rd SUFFOLK
8am 24th
3·20am 24th
8am 24th
NORFOLK
2 10am 24th
Midnight
11pm 23rd
BISMARCK & PRINZ EUGEN 7·22 pm 23rd
British Minefield
HOOD SUNK 6am 24th
6am 24th
12·17am 24th
7·22 pm 23rd
CONVOY S.C.31 8am 24th
HOOD, PRINCE OF WALES & 6 DESTROYERS
ICELAND
CONVOY HX126 8am 24th
4·10am 24th
ARETHUSA
5 TRAWLERS
MANCHESTER
BIRMINGHAM
8·32 pm 23rd NORFOLK'S SIGHTING REPORT RECEIVED BY C in C
8pm 23rd
RODNEY LEAVES BRITANNIC
FAEROE IS
RODNEY & 4 DESTROYERS ESCORTING BRITANNIC
KING GEORGE V (C in C H.F) VICTORIOUS, REPULSE, GALATEA AURORA, KENYA, HERMIONE, & 7 DESTROYERS
CONVOY OB 325 8am 24th
8am 23rd
7·10am 23rd REPULSE (from CLYDE) JOINS C.in C
CONVOY WS8B 8am 24th ESCORTED BY EXETER CAIRO & 8 DESTROYERS (SAILED CLYDE 22nd)
CONVOY OB 326 8am 24th.
ORKNEYS
SHETLAND IS
HOME FLEET SAILS 10·45pm 22nd.
IRELAND
SCOTLAND

Lieutenant N. N. Goddard, R.N.V.R., and as observer, Commander G. A. Rotherham, R.N. Commander Rotherham had many years of flying to his credit, and had acquired the very necessary experience for this type of work.

Captain Fancourt received approval for the mission from his Commander-in-Chief and from Coastal Command. The aircraft took off late in the afternoon of May 22. It flew low across the North Sea, at times literally skimming the wave tops, in the popular phrase of that day—"with nothing on the clock but the maker's name." The cloud base was right down, and even at sea level the visibility was poor. Commander Rotherham used the old navigator's trick of making a deliberate error—instead of attempting to lay a course for Bergen direct, he aimed for a point to the south of it. In this way he would know, when the aircraft reached the coast, that he had only to turn north and sooner or later he would sight his objective. Skimming and climbing, coming down to check wind velocity at sea level, and then lifting again to two or three thousand feet, the aircraft swept across the North Sea, like a pebble skipping over a lake. It was a magnificent feat of air skill and navigation, carried out under conditions which had kept all other aircraft blind and tied down to their stations.

At 7:39 P.M. in the evening, Hatston Air Station reported to the Commander-in-Chief:

"Following received from Hatston reconnaissance aircraft over Bergen. Battleship and cruiser have left."

Commander Rotherham and his pilot had done it. After finding the coast, they had flown along it to Bergen. They had seen that the harbor was empty. While every gun on ship and shore had let fly at them, they had circled the fiord to confirm their first judgment, had come out low over the roof tops in a hail of fire, and headed for home.

Within three minutes of receiving the signal from Hatston, Admiral Tovey made to his ships in company: "Prepare for sea."

It was now nearly 8 P.M., and the fleet were at two hours' notice for steam. They would be ready to weigh anchor at 10 P.M. The Suffolk was told to reinforce the Norfolk in the Denmark Strait, the Arethusa to join the Birmingham and Manchester in the Iceland-Faeroes passage, and Admiral Holland in the Hood was told—instead of proceeding to Hvalfiord to fuel—to cover the area to the southwestward of Iceland. The Hood and the Prince of Wales must be at hand should the enemy break out, either through the Denmark Strait, or through the Iceland-Faeroes passage. Admiral Tovey also requested air reconnaissance to be maintained over:

(*a*) Iceland-Faeroes channel.
(*b*) Denmark Strait.
(*c*) Faeroes-Shetland channel.
(*d*) Norwegian coast.

He now knew that the Bismarck and the cruiser had sailed. What he did not know was whether they were in fact heading for an Atlantic breakout, or whether they might not be on their way back to the Baltic. He assumed, however, that the worst had happened.

Shortly before 9 P.M. Sir John Tovey made a further signal:

"I intend to proceed in King George V with Victorious, Galatea, Hermione, Kenya, Aurora, and seven destroyers, passing through Hoxa boom at 2300 Thursday 22 May. . . ."

The Repulse, on passage up from the Clyde, was ordered to join the Commander-in-Chief by noon on May 23.

By midnight, the Commander-in-Chief and his ships were steaming hard through the dark eddies of the Pentland Firth. Far to the north of them the Hood, the Prince of Wales, and their six destroyers were slicing through the night. Admiral Lutjens and his two ships were headed northwest toward the Arctic Circle. At his present speed he would be nearing the entrance to the Denmark Strait by the evening of the twenty-third.

19

The Denmark Strait

A savage area of ice and mist, frost smoke and water-skies, the Denmark Strait has a haunted air. Separating Greenland from Iceland, it is only 150 miles wide at the point where Horn, the northern cape of Iceland, juts out into the sea.

Off Horn itself, a British mine field stretched out in a northwesterly direction. It was a declared mine field: we had published the fact that the area was dangerous to shipping, although we had not, of course, stated the exact area in which our mines were laid. But the Germans were perfectly capable of assessing their probably extent, from the charted depth of the water. They had already passed a number of ships through the Strait and out into the Atlantic, among them the merchant raider Atlantis on April 7, 1940, the Orion on April 9, and the raiders Widder, Thor, and Pinguin in May and June. On October 27, 1940, the Admiral Scheer had also made her way into the Atlantic by this route.

Sir John Tovey's assessment that the Denmark Strait was the most probable route for the Bismarck and Prinz Eugen to take was to be confirmed. Although the passage at this time of the year was narrow, weather conditions were such that air patrols were unlikely to be of much assistance, and visibility at sea level was almost equally unreliable.

On the eastern side of the Strait, the coastal waters of Iceland remain free of ice, under the influence of the Irminger current. This current, a branch of the warm North Atlantic current (which stems from the Gulf Stream), divides southwest of Iceland. One part of it flows up Iceland's western coast, and keeps this area navigable at all seasons of the year.

On the western side of the Denmark Strait, the barren shores of Greenland remain unaffected by the current, and great areas of the coast line are fringed by a border of eternal ice. During the winter months this ice spreads out across the Strait reducing the navigable width from something like ninety miles in August to forty or forty-five miles in April and May. At the period of the Bismarck's passage through the Strait, it was estimated that between the ice edge and the northern cape of Iceland, the area of open water extended about sixty miles. Off Horn itself the navigable channel was somewhat less, for our moored mines had closed the jaws of the ice-free water.

The northwestern coast of Iceland, off which Norfolk and Suffolk had their patrol ground, is a place of austere beauty. The land here is a peninsula formed by the deep bays of Breidhafjördur and Hunaflói. On the western side, it is pierced by the deep scars of lonely fiords. In places there are narrow coastal strips, sparsely inhabited, but mostly the land plummets into the sea from heights of 2,000 feet and more. Basalt, a somber rock, predominates and makes the fiord entrances look like black tunnels against the winter snowfields of the mountain peaks.

"Iceland is the best land on which the sun shines," runs a local proverb. It is a harsh country, but with a curious beauty that sets it apart from anywhere else in the world.

And through the drifts the snowy cliffs
Did send a dismal sheen. . . .

But when the light catches the distant peaks they shine like a remote Valhalla—a fitting place for Viking gods and heroes.

There are strange sounds in the island, sounds which break the needle-sharp silence of the northern night. Sometimes a rock splits, or a long sighing fall tells of the winter snow clearing from a high peak. In the old days these noises were believed to be caused by the trolls, as they worked in their secret mountain caves, forging unconquerable swords and deathless axes. One might imagine that the shades of the old Icelandic poets gathered on that May morning and stared seaward from frozen headland or cold sea strand. They would have understood this great drama—a battle of long ships in the light of a northern dawn.

There were other hazards in the Strait, not only ice and mine field. Mirage is frequent in that crisp air and the light plays funny tricks on strained eyes. Ships seem to change course suddenly, or even disappear into a clear horizon. "Skip distances" in the visibility, followed by snow flurries in which all sight is lost, confuse the lookouts. Mist sweeps up from the sea and then lifts again as inexplicably as it has come. When the wind blows from the northwest over the ice, frost smoke develops—pale opalescent clouds caused by the passage of cold air over the warm current. An acid-white glare in the sky, the reflection of pack ice on a low cloud base, produces the phenomenon known as "ice blink." At the same time an ocherish reflection, "land blink," may rise above the distant land.

Sometimes sailors on patrol would catch glimpses of the far-off nunataks of Greenland, lonely peaks shining against a pale blue sky. Sea smoke fumed over the coastal water. Flickering above the ice, dark patches of water-sky were visible wherever a reflection of open sea was cast on the cloud base. Sometimes a sleet or snow storm would hurl down and darken the sailors' watching world. When the ships stood over toward the ice edge, they would cut their way through the scum of frazil crystals—thin plates of ice floating wherever the sea was on the point of freezing. Here, the water would have a dead, oily appearance, and the wind that bit the sailors' faces would hardly ruffle the surface.

On May 23, 1940, the Denmark Strait was calm, and the visibility to the north was clear. A light air was lifting down over the ice and causing the faintest of ripples on the sea. There was practically no swell. The cold air flowing over the warm Irminger current set up a heavy fog, and in the direction of Iceland the visibility was down to zero. There was a curious contrast between the bright sky over the ice, the narrow pathway of open water, and the heavy fog bank running almost parallel to the ice edge.

It was under these conditions that the cruisers Norfolk and Suffolk were carrying out their patrol. It was into this twilight world that the Bismarck and Prinz Eugen were steaming. Far to the south of them Admiral Holland's force was headed north toward their patrol ground.

20

Enemy in Sight

Luck seemed to be on the side of Admiral Lutjens. Throughout the day of the twenty-third, weather conditions deteriorated. The wind came from the east, the wind off the cold mountains of Norway which raises mist as it passes over the sea. Rain came up with the mist, and at times the visibility was little more than a hundred yards. The weather which so favored the German breakout had one advantage for the British. Although it prevented their own air patrols from operating efficiently, it also prevented German reconnaissance from discovering that Scapa Flow was empty. Admiral Lutjens knew that he had been sighted in Bergen, but not that every available unit of the Home Fleet was steaming hard to cut off his escape.

If the German Admiral could take comfort from the thick weather, Admiral Tovey felt himself increasingly hampered. At 6:30 A.M. he received the signal: "From Admiral, Rosyth: air reconnaissance postponed owing to weather." He had lost his westerly defensive reconnaissance. Worse still, the Norwegian coast patrol, which might have told him whether the German ships were in fact tucked away in another fiord, or homeward bound for Germany, could not be flown. The Denmark Strait was also unwatched, and only the Iceland-Faeroes patrol was maintained throughout the day. The air patrol of the Faeroes–Shetland channel had to be abandoned shortly after noon. Admiral Tovey had only the eyes of his surface ships upon which to rely—and they were thinly dispersed.

Radar was still in its infancy, and although the gunnery sets which had now been installed in most of the fleet units were efficient up to ten or eleven miles range, they were not ideal for searching. In the Iceland–Faeroes passage, the three cruisers were each covering a patrol line of nearly a hundred miles. On a day of good visibility their maximum visual range would be about twenty miles. But in this weather a large area was left that could not be watched.

In the Denmark Strait, Rear-Admiral W. F. Wake-Walker, in his flagship the Norfolk, had to contend with the unusual conditions which have been described. He had now been joined by Captain R. M. Ellis in the Suffolk, who had been instructed to patrol northeast and southwest along the edge of the Greenland ice pack. The Norfolk was patrolling deep in the mist twelve to fifteen miles south of the Suffolk, who was in the clear, mist-free lane of water that bordered the ice.

Both ships were fitted with radar, but the set installed in the Suffolk was of an improved type that could be trained to cover all angles of bearing, except across the stern. Rear-Admiral Wake-Walker's flagship was fitted with the earlier gunnery radar set, which was unrotatable, covering only a comparatively small arc directly ahead of the vessel. For the purposes of search or shadowing, the Suffolk was clearly a more efficient ship, and her efficiency was increased by the fact that her captain had taken a personal interest in the possibilities of radar. A cruiser's purpose is not to engage enemy capital ships, but to shadow and "sick on" to them her own capital ships. Captain Ellis knew that the improved radar set fitted to his ship made her almost twice as efficient as she had been. No longer was she blind, even when in mist or fog or darkness.

The Hood and the Prince of Wales were now almost on their patrol line, slightly to the southwest of Reykjanes. A long way south of them, the Commander-in-Chief was steering northwest, his ships bumping heavily into an increasing swell. The destroyers staggered and lurched, and the great bows of the Victorious rose and fell with endless monotony.

The day wore on, and still there was no news of the enemy. The few air patrols that could be flown had nothing to report, and Admiral Tovey and his staff felt the strain increase with every hour that passed. There was always the possibility that the enemy might by now be steaming into position to launch an assault on the Faeroes, far to the east of them. There was also the chance that he might have slipped through the cruiser patrol lines overnight, and be through the Iceland–Faeroes channel—escaping south of Admiral Holland and north of Admiral Tovey. Hood and the ships in company with her lay well to the west, it was true, but unless the enemy passed within fifteen miles of them they might never be sighted. A signal from "Admiral, Iceland," at 6:17 P.M. did little to dissipate the gloom:

"Study of recent air reconnaissance shows that a well-built ship could make a passage through Denmark Strait about 50 miles inside ice edge."

Was it possible that while the Norfolk and Suffolk were patrolling in the clear water, somewhere far to the north of them the Bismarck and her cruiser escort were slipping through the pack leads, unwatched, and hampered only by the growl and crackle of ice at their bows?

The northern twilight began to fall. It was 7 P.M. The Norfolk was patrolling in the thick mist that ran all the way south to the Icelandic shores, the Suffolk was on her southwesterly course. It was this leg of his patrol which caused her captain the greatest uneasiness. His radar was blind over the stern, and it was from that direction—from the northeast—that the enemy was most likely to appear. With this in mind, he had put additional lookouts on the after-bearings. Hunched in their duffel coats, slapping their gloved hands together (and longing for eight o'clock, when the second dogwatch would be over and their reliefs appear), the seamen strained their eyes toward the northern approaches to the Denmark Strait. The ice edge was pink and blue under the declining sun, and the ship's wake was very clear against the gun-metal sea.

At 7:22 P.M. there was a shout from Able Seaman Newell, the starboard after lookout.

"Ship bearing Green One Four Oh degrees!"

The air seemed to give a snap, as if a current of electricity had been released. Captain Ellis and the officers on the bridge rushed to the side. Even before they had got their binoculars to their eyes, the report was corrected:

"Two ships bearing Green One Four Oh!"

There they were! In that split second Captain Ellis had seen the battleship Bismarck and the heavy cruiser Prinz Eugen bearing down toward him—less than 14,000 yards away, point-blank range for a 15-inch gun.

The Captain's reaction was automatic.

"Hard a-port!"

The helmsman spun the wheel. The Suffolk leaned over so that in the messdecks cups, knives, and forks cascaded down the tables. As the cruiser's bows slid into the enveloping mist there was a sigh of relief. The range had been only seven miles, yet the Germans had failed to see them. Even before she had escaped into the welcome obscurity a message was on its way from the W/T office.

"From Suffolk to Norfolk.

"One battleship, one cruiser in sight bearing 020 degrees distant 7 miles. Course 240 degrees."

Immediately on receiving the signal, Captain A. J. L. Phillips in the Norfolk altered course to close the enemy's estimated position. He was deep in the fog bank and if, as he expected, the enemy was making the passage of the Strait at high speed, he must use every available ounce of power to get into his shadowing position on her quarter.

Meanwhile the Suffolk, after her withdrawal into the fog bank, had maneuvered in order to allow the enemy to pass her. Those were anxious moments, for no one could be sure that the Germans did not possess efficient gunnery radar sets. If they did, the first—and perhaps the last—thing the Suffolk would know about it would be the scream of a 15-inch salvo. As soon as the Bismarck and the Prinz Eugen began to draw forward off his beam, Captain Ellis took up station on their port quarter. The Suffolk followed as the radar operator watched the German ships on his screen. She kept at a distance of twelve to thirteen miles, the limit of her radar. The Germans were steaming at high speed, 28 to 30 knots. The Suffolk, hanging on their tail, continued to report their movements.

The Commander-in-Chief was not yet aware that the enemy had been found. A defect in the Suffolk's W/T transmissions (probably caused by damp in the aerial trunking, for it wore off later and her transmissions were received) had resulted in the fact that only her sister ship, the Norfolk, was so far aware of the enemy's presence in the Denmark Strait. Between her first sighting of the Bismarck and 6 A.M. the following morning, the Suffolk, in fact, made thirty reports of the enemy's course and speed.

It was a little over a quarter of an hour later, at 7:39 P.M., that Admiral Holland aboard the Hood received one of the Suffolk's reports. He and his force were almost due south of the enemy, and only about 300 miles away. Provided the cruisers could keep in touch throughout the night, there was little doubt that the Hood and the Prince of Wales would be able to bring the enemy to battle early in the morning. The Admiral immediately signalled his force to increase to 27 knots and turned to a course of 295 degrees to intercept. With the increase in speed the tremor of the ships' hulls mounted, the thunder of the broken water at their bows redoubled, and the word went through the ships. "Suffolk's found 'em. Denmark Strait."

At 8:30 P.M. the Norfolk suddenly emerged at full speed from the blanket of mist, to find the Bismarck and Prinz Eugen on her port bow, uncomfortably close—the range being about six miles. The ships were almost on reciprocal courses and the range was coming down rapidly. The Germans were not caught unaware a second time, and Norfolk was less lucky than her sister ship. Even as Captain Phillips ordered the wheel hard-a-starboard, the Bismarck's guns opened fire. The Norfolk was swinging back as fast as she could go toward the sheltering edge of mist, and the buzzer from bridge to engine room "make smoke" was answered by thick oily clouds rolling from her funnel. Even so the cruiser came under a heavy and accurate fire—a foretaste of the efficiency of German gunnery. Now the Norfolk's company heard that harsh ripping sound—like a gigantic sheet tearing—which marks the flight of heavy shells. Vast columns of water sprang into the air to port and starboard of the cruiser as a quick-fired series of three 15-inch salvos fell all round her. The whine of flying steel followed the thunder of bursting shells, and splinters from near misses fell aboard. Snaking away at full speed, her smoke hanging heavy over the ruffled sea behind her, the Norfolk regained the mist in safety.

At 8:32 P.M. she made her first enemy report: "One battleship one cruiser in sight. . . ." and it was this which gave the Commander-in-Chief his first news of the Bismarck's presence in the Denmark Strait. When the message was received the King George V was about 600 miles southeast of the enemy. The fleet's course was slightly north of west. If the Germans turned to the south the King George V would be waiting for them.

The six destroyers escorting the Hood and the Prince of Wales were making heavy weather of it in the increasing sea. At 8:55 P.M. Admiral Holland signaled them: "If you are unable to maintain this speed I will have to go on without you. You should follow at your best speed."

The spray was breaking over the destroyers' bridges, and their foredecks were afoam with the press of water. They held on. No destroyer man likes to feel that he cannot keep pace with a battleship, even in heavy weather. They would accept some superficial damage to boats and gear rather than be left behind at such a moment.

At that time of the year the Arctic twilight lasts almost all night. There is a period of about five hours comparative darkness, but the sun is never far below the horizon. Although the night of May 23/24 was darker than usual, there was hardly more than a brief period of real dark. Through this eerie twilight hunters and hunted, pursuers and pursued, tore through the icy Denmark Strait; the Bismarck and Prinz Eugen, bent on making their escape into the Atlantic before British heavy forces could intercept them; the two cruisers hanging on their heels like wolves.

The main danger to the shadowing ships was that Admiral Lutjens, aware that the British cruisers were following him, might suddenly reverse his course and, with a 180-degree turn, hurl himself at the light ships and destroy them. Such a move was more than a probability, it was almost to be expected, and Norfolk and Suffolk were all the time acutely aware of this danger. Previous sorties by German warships, on the other hand, had shown that they were unwilling to accept an action, even against inferior warships. One may suppose that Admiral Lutjens did not turn back because he was bent at all costs on making a speedy escape into the Atlantic. Apart from which, although he had sighted only one cruiser, he could not be sure that there were no other British ships—possibly heavy ships—steaming hard after him through the fog. In the event, he kept his course, hoping no doubt that in the difficult conditions of the Arctic twilight he would be able to shake off his shadowers.

It was now that the strange conditions of the Strait began to afflict the cruisers. Blinding flurries of snow whipped over the ice edge. Rain storms and mist patches were errant on the sea, and, had it not been for their radar sets, the British ships might well have lost touch with the enemy. They were also aware that the farther down the Denmark Strait the chase continued, the more the water opened out to starboard, giving the Bismarck greater freedom to maneuver. At the moment she, like themselves, was constrained by the closeness of the ice edge, and had little opportunity for large-scale alterations of course, except to port.

The cruisers were maintaining their watch at a range of some twelve miles, a distance from which they were also intermittently in visual contact with the enemy. It was now that, in addition to its snow and rain, the Strait produced another hazard for the lookouts in the form of mirage. There was one moment when the watchers on the Suffolk's bridge were convinced that the battleship had altered course toward them. Immediately, the cruiser's wheel was put hard over and she reversed her course. In the circumstances—and everyone was certain that they had seen the silhouette of the battleship alter round—it was the obvious thing to do. If the ships had been on reciprocal courses, with a combined approach speed of about 56 knots, the battleship would have been hard on the Suffolk, with a 15-inch salvo in the air, in a matter of minutes. But when the radar range faded and there was no sign of the battleship, the Suffolk's bridge realized that their eyes had played them tricks. Again she reversed course and increased to full speed to make good the four miles or more that she had lost.

At 10:56 P.M. that evening, Admiral Tovey signaled the cruiser Galatea: "I am hoping Hood may head them off and force them to turn back or to the southward. . . ."

At 12:15 A.M., 0015 on the morning of May 24, Admiral Holland made the long-expected signal to his ships in company, and to his own men: "Prepare for action."

In the cold of the northern night, battle ensigns were hoisted: the large white ensigns which fly from the masts of H.M. ships only when action with the enemy is imminent. As they were run up the darkened yards they strained and lifted on their halyards, then streamed aft in the wind of the ships' passing. From the spray-swept bridges of the bucketing destroyers, captains and officers turned their eyes toward the Hood and the Prince of Wales. They could see the flicker of their battle ensigns against the midnight sky.

21

"Prepare for Action!"

As midnight approached in the Denmark Strait, the wind brought up the snow, and visual contact with the enemy was lost. Now the worst happened—the Suffolk lost radar contact. For nearly three hours the Commander-in-Chief in the King George V and Vice-Admiral Holland in the Hood listened out anxiously for news from the north. No signals came through from the two cruisers.

Just before midnight the Bismarck had disappeared into a snowstorm. The clutter on the radar scan, due to the thick snow, was no help to the Suffolk's radar operator. Shortly after losing sight of the Bismarck, when the Suffolk herself was blanketed by snow, she lost all contact.

During this period, Admiral Holland altered his squadron's course. The lack of news presented the Admiral with an extremely difficult problem. If, as it appeared, the enemy had succeeded in eluding the cruisers—what action might one expect her to take? The Hood and the Prince of Wales had been steering to intercept the enemy, provided that he maintained his course of southwest. But, knowing that he was being shadowed, it was reasonable to expect Admiral Lutjens to make a major alteration overnight in order to throw off his pursuers. During those hours when no signals came through from the Suffolk, it seemed as if he had succeeded in doing this. The edge of the Greenland ice pack on Admiral Lutjens' starboard hand would prevent him from making any large alterations of course toward the west. The most likely conclusion, therefore, was that he had come more southerly; either to due south, or a little east of south. If this were the case, Admiral Holland's course to intercept must be modified. His main objective was still to bring his squadron to battle with the enemy in the shortest possible time, but he was now also faced with a search problem. At 12:17 A.M., accordingly, the signal was made from the Hood for the squadron to reduce speed to 25 knots, and to alter course to due north. If the enemy had turned to the south, this would have put the Hood and the Prince of Wales in a good position to intercept the Bismarck.

It is always easy to be wise after the event. The senior officers, writers, and critics who seize their pens as soon as peace breaks out, and describe why or how campaigns were fought (or should have been fought) are apt to forget the way in which things really happened. It is difficult to attempt an assessment of what passed through the minds of Admiral Holland and his staff during those hours. There are no records, only a few signals. The Admiral was an able commander, who had already proved his efficiency in the Mediterranean theater, and who was regarded—as his promotion to Second-in-Command of the Home Fleet testifies—as one of the most competent senior offiicers in the service. It is not easy to visualize the situation as it may have appeared to him. But one must try to bear in mind the climate of action, those long hours when tiredness and tension have taken their toll.

Only Tolstoy has written with complete truthfulness about war.

> But all these hints of foresight are now brought forward . . . because the events have justified them. If the event had not

> taken place, these hints would have been forgotten, like thousands and millions of contrary hints and suppositions, which then were current, but have proved incorrect, and so have been forgotten. For the issue of any event there are always so many suppositions that, no matter how it may end, there will always be found people who will say, "I told you then that it would end so," forgetting entirely that in the endless mass of suppositions made, there were some that were diametrically opposed.

Admiral Holland's guess that the Bismarck and Prinz Eugen had turned to the south was incorrect. Had it been correct, and had the outcome of the action been different, he would have been hailed as a brilliant commander, and there was in fact every good reason for thinking that since the Bismarck had eluded our cruisers, she had done so by an alteration to the south.

Napoleon required that his marshals should be lucky, and in this, at any rate, he was astute. Luck is what admirals and generals need above all, for with it they may lead the triumph wreathed in laurels. Men more able than they perhaps—but without luck—are left behind as the "small change" on the battlefield. Admiral Holland's alteration of course meant that when contact was finally regained with the enemy, his squadron was no longer so well placed for making an interception. He was not lucky.

Below decks in the Hood and the Prince of Wales nearly three thousand men were closed up at their action stations. Admiral Holland's original estimation had been that the enemy might be sighted any time after 1:40 A.M., and from 12:30 onward the tension of impending action invaded the ships. Turrets turned, guns elevated, and directors swiveled and focused like giant eyes. At such a moment a warship fuses into one unit. . . .

At 2:10 A.M., Admiral Holland altered course to the southeast. If the enemy—as he assumed—had eluded the Norfolk and Suffolk by altering to the south, he wanted to maintain his position well on their bow. To continue farther on his northerly course might well have put him too far ahead, so that he would have lost a lot of bearing on an enemy headed south. As the Hood and the Prince of Wales altered course, the Admiral dispatched his destroyers to the north. The most vital object at that moment was to re-establish contact with the enemy. The dispatch of his destroyers to sweep northward—since he had assumed that the Bismarck might be heading in this direction—was a logical step.

Throughout those long hours of waiting, the Hood and the Prince of Wales maintained radar silence. Admiral Holland has been criticized for adopting this policy. Yet, even if the Hood and the Prince of Wales had used their radar sets, it would have made no difference to the final outcome. The Bismarck was far to the north of them and outside radar range.

Admiral Holland's objective was to bring the enemy to battle with every advantage of surprise. He was well aware that if the Germans were to detect radar impulses coming from the south of them (and not only from the shadowing cruisers astern), they might guess that these emanated from British capital ships racing to head them off. Recent experience with the battle cruisers Scharnhorst and Gneisenau had shown that German surface ships were under orders to avoid action with British fleet units at all costs. It was not to be presumed that Admiral Lutjens, if he knew that capital ships were moving up from the south of him, would stand and fight. The most reasonable assumption was that he would turn about, and escape back through the Denmark Strait.

At 2:47 A.M. the news came through:

"They've found them again."

The relief felt by both Admiral Tovey and Admiral Holland can be imagined. The enemy had not doubled back on her tracks: she had not sunk the shadowing cruisers; she had not eluded them; she was still maintaining her same course and speed—still headed for the Atlantic. The Hood and the Prince of Wales immediately swung back to the northward, and increased speed to 28 knots.

The news was soon confirmed by further reports. These enabled the plotting officers in the Hood and the Prince of Wales to bring their operations plot up to date.

The knowledge that the Bismarck was in the Denmark Strait had already had its effect on our shipping in the Atlantic. Convoys were being rerouted, and Vice-Admiral Somerville's Force H, which had left Gibraltar at 2 A.M., had been ordered to cover a troop convoy then passing through the Bay of Biscay. Force H, in which Hood had once played a leading role, now consisted of the battle cruiser Renown, the cruiser Sheffield, and six destroyers. The Hood's old "chummy ship," the Ark Royal, still formed the kernel of Force H's offensive power. In mid-Atlantic the battleship Ramillies was escorting a westbound convoy. The battleship Rodney was also in the Atlantic, headed toward America for a long-overdue refit. The battleship Revenge was in Halifax, Nova Scotia. All these ships were acquainted with the news, and the Admiralty earmarked them for use against the Bismarck, should the necessity arise.

Meanwhile Admiral Lutjens continued his steady course southwestward. The Prinz Eugen was leading the Bismarck, and from a distance they might easily have been taken for sister ships. The silhouettes of the German vessels were very similar. The German naval constructors tended to work to an overall plan of design—whether they were building a heavy cruiser or a battleship—in which the same features were repeated. The fact that the Prinz Eugen was in the van, rather than the Bismarck, and the similarity of the silhouettes of the two ships, would play an important part in the action that was to follow.

In Admiral Lutjens' flagship there was a feeling of cheerful confidence. Even the sailors knew, of course, that they had been sighted by a British cruiser on the previous evening. They had seen their shells falling round the Norfolk and had watched her escape into the mist. It had also been announced over their ship's broadcasting system that the cruiser had radioed the Bismarck's position. Yet, even so, they had no suspicion that there were any

British capital ships in the vicinity. To the Admiral and his staff it seemed that they had merely been unfortunate in running into a British cruiser patrol. By the time any heavy ships could get north from Scapa Flow to try and head them off, the Bismarck should be well out into the North Atlantic. The "unsinkable Bismarck," she had been called, and her officers knew that, ship for ship, she was a match for any vessel in the world. They had no knowledge of the dispatch with which Admiral Tovey had sailed the Hood and the Prince of Wales—even before he had definitely known that the Bismarck was out. A seaman aboard the Bismarck, in a statement made later,* said that after the ship's company had been told that the enemy cruiser had radioed the Bismarck's position ". . . it was announced that the enemy cruisers were shooting at each other. After that we were relieved. The night was quiet." Presumably this piece of wishful thinking was given out to raise the spirits of the German crew—not that either their morale or their efficiency was low, as they were later to prove. A great many of them, though, were new to active operations. The Bismarck was carrying a number of young officers and men from her sister ship, the Tirpitz, who had been sent aboard for training and sea experience. This gave her a total complement of nearly twenty-four hundred men.

From 3 A.M. onward the visibility began to improve. The wind was a little north of east and there was a moderate swell running, as the Hood and the Prince of Wales steamed through the brightening sea. They were alone. The destroyers were still sweeping to the north.

It is difficult to see why Vice-Admiral Holland did not recall his destroyers, now that he knew the Bismarck had not altered course. One can only conjecture that he expected her to make a drastic turn to port and attempt to escape immediately she saw the two British capital ships approaching. The reluctance of other German capital ships to be brought to battle had made

*Martienssen, *Hitler and His Admirals*.

such a move on her part more than likely. Admiral Holland knew that the Bismarck had probably a knot or two in hand over his own ship and the Prince of Wales, and that if she attempted flight she might well get away. If she had altered to port, either back through the Denmark Strait or away to the south of Iceland, the six destroyers positioned to the north of Admiral Holland might have been in a position to attack with torpedoes, or—at the least—to maintain contact with her. Once again, the Admiral was not so much unskillful as he was unlucky.

22

Death of a Giant

The brief darkness began to lift soon after 2 A.M. The cloud base as it raced by overhead started to break up, revealing individual clouds, pennants and streamers of cirrus, with here and there heavier patches of nimbus, the rain bearer. The surface of the sea, which all night had raced past their bows in a dark violence, became patterned with waves—no longer a blind moving mass, but separate and distinct crests. The swell lifted and slopped from the northeast, and broke sucking against the ship's sides. The sea began to glow like old silver, and the stars were dying.

Through the northern dawn, seven thousand men were hurling toward each other, unaware as yet of each other's existence. Their eyes were fixed upon instruments and counters, their hands busy upon levers and control wheels, and their bodies swaying gently to the scend of the sea. At 3:40 A.M. Admiral Holland had turned more northerly in order to make his interception. The two ships were steaming at 28 knots and their bows were bumping into the sea. The spray rose flickering in great sheets above the long sheer of the Hood's fo'c's'le, to fall with a crash over the sweep of the steel deck. It beat against the armored face of "A" and "B" turrets, and swept against the bridge.

Steaming cups of cocoa were passed round the lookouts. Many

of the men had spent all night at their action stations. They slept huddled up in duffel coats, their heads pillowed on life belts. Inside the ship, the shine of long lines of lights, the winking of dials and indicators, and the steady murmur of machinery created a special world, remote from the dawn that was breaking outside. No scent of the night sea, the clean tang of wet decks, or of the salt spray drying and dripping on bridge or boatdeck, could be detected down below. In this great city, the lights still shone as they had always shone. Only the sense of some special tension in the air made things seem any different from a hundred and one other patrols.

By 4 A.M., the visibility was about ten miles, and it was estimated that the Bismarck was some twenty miles to the northeast of the squadron. Shortly after 4:30 A.M. the Prince of Wales began to prepare her aircraft, with a view to flying it off for reconnaissance. But the spray, which had been drenching the ship, had contaminated the petrol. Hands were still working to clear the fuel supply when it became obvious that action would be joined before the aircraft could be launched. (The aircraft was jettisoned within a minute of fire having been opened.)

Admiral Lutjens and his squadron were sliding out of the night and the north, closed up in readiness, and yet with the comfortable feeling that they had almost eluded the British. The cruisers, they knew, were still there, somewhere astern of them; but the Bismarck and Prinz Eugen were now almost clear of the dangerous narrow Strait. Soon they would be able to take violent evasive action.

The Norfolk and Suffolk hung grimly on their heels. The first part of their mission had been successfully carried out. They had found the enemy and had continued to pass the news of his course and speed to their Commander-in-Chief. They did not yet know how far away were the nearest British heavy ships. They might still have another whole day of shadowing before them, shadowing which would grow increasingly difficult as the constraint of the Greenland ice pack gradually receded.

It was not until 4:45 A.M. that the cruisers intercepted a signal from one of Admiral Holland's destroyers, who were still patrolling to the north of the Hood and the Prince of Wales. Now they learned that British capital ships were in the area.

"We suddenly realized that we were going to have a front-row seat in the stalls!" They could little have guessed the nature of the tragedy they would witness.

At 5:15 A.M. a stir of excitement ran through the men in the cruisers. Lifting over the horizon on their port bow were two dark smudges of smoke. There could be nothing else in those latitudes which would be heading northward but heavy units of the Home Fleet. Only heavy units steaming at full speed would raise such smoke clouds.

A few minutes before the Hood and the Prince of Wales were sighted by the cruisers, the signal "Instant readiness for action" had been made by Admiral Holland. All night long, as they raced northward, the men had been waiting for this moment. Now, a long sigh seemed to echo through the two warships. After all the preparation, the checking, and the counterchecking, the actual signal that action was imminent seemed to release the tension and quiet the nerves. The great guns and turrets turned as the crews followed their pointers. Beneath their feet the hydraulic machinery gave its grunting hiss as the gun muzzles lifted. The petty officer watching the hydraulic pressure gave a thumbs-up signal to the gunner's mate: "Everything okay!"

Admiral Holland's intention had been to make an almost end-on approach, fine on the enemy's port bow, and to close the range as quickly as possible before turning his two ships so that their broadsides could be brought to bear.* His alteration of course during the night, when the enemy had been lost to our

*For an analysis of the action, see pages 210-219.

cruisers, had cost him much of his advantage. When, at 5:35, the two ships were sighted seventeen miles away on the starboard bow, he had lost a lot of his bearing on the enemy.

Immediately on sighting the dim shapes on the horizon, the forward turrets of the Hood and the Prince of Wales swung round. The muzzles of the guns lifted. Except for the sound of the sea breaking, and the crackle of orders and reports over telephones, a great silence seemed to enfold the ships.

At 5:37 A.M. an enemy sighting report—"Distant 17 miles"—was sent out from the Prince of Wales, to be followed at 5:44 by one from the Hood—"Distant 14 miles." Two minutes later Admiral Holland turned his two ships 40 degrees toward the enemy. His intention was to shorten the range. Inevitably, this meant that the "A" arcs were closed—that the after turrets of the Hood and the Prince of Wales were no longer able to bear on the target.

The Admiral had two good reasons for wishing to get in as close as possible, before using the advantage of the greater broadsides available to him. He knew the weakness of his own ship—her deck armor—the greater the range, therefore, the greater was the likelihood of the Hood being hit by a plummeting shell. At closer range, where the shell's trajectory would be flatter, he knew that the Hood's vertical armor should be able to withstand punishment. He had also to bear in mind the weak points of the Prince of Wales. She was not properly "worked up," and therefore could not be counted upon as thoroughly efficient in her gunnery. Another thing must have worried him—the known teething troubles in her turrets, and the fact that contractors' workmen were at that moment still working on them. Furthermore, one of the Prince of Wales's forward guns was defective. It would be able to fire in only the first salvo before becoming inoperative. In these circumstances, to close the range must have seemed the most sensible, if not the only, course.

At 5:30, Admiral Lutjens had also sighted the smoke to the south. Action stations sounded in the Bismarck, and the Admiral waited with impatience for the reports from his spotting officers. The ships were closing him rapidly, almost end-on. The first reports suggested that they were British heavy cruisers. For a second he must have hesitated. But he had nearly won out into the Atlantic now, and the temptation to go on was irresistible.

Admiral Holland intended to carry out the action in close order, both ships being maneuvered together as one unit. They were now turned a further 20 degrees toward the enemy. Their speed was still 28 knots, and the range was coming down fast. Except for the swell, the sea was fairly calm. The funnel smoke shivered high in the air over the Hood's boatdeck and trailed aft to hang darkly over her wake. Astern of her, at a distance of 800 yards, the Prince of Wales followed.

At 5:52 A.M. the range was 25,000 yards, when the circuits were closed. The ding! ding! of the fire gong sounded in the Hood. It pricked the bubble of silence. Admiral Lutjens now realized that his first assessment had been wrong—these were no cruisers! At the same moment he signaled, "Am engaging two heavy units." Dark-brownish cordite clouds lifted on the horizon and the air was torn apart by the scream of 15-inch salvos.

At 1:47 A.M. that morning Admiral Holland had signaled his tactical intentions to Captain Leach in the Prince of Wales. Both ships would concentrate their fire on the Bismarck. The heavy cruiser they would leave to the care of the Norfolk and Suffolk. At 5:49 A.M. he signaled for a concentration of fire on the leading ship. The similarity of the two silhouettes had deceived the Admiral into assuming her to be the Bismarck. But, aboard the Prince of Wales, Captain Leach and his gunnery officer were convinced that the Bismarck was the second ship. They had already decided to disregard Admiral Holland's signal when, at 5:52, he made to them "Shift target right." At the very moment of opening fire the Admiral had realized his mistake.

The Hood fired first. She was followed a second later by the Bismarck, and then by the Prince of Wales. Within one minute, at a range of about 25,000 yards, all three ships had opened fire.

> The thundering line of battle stands,
> And in the air Death moans and sings. . . .

Now, all about the ships, the sea broke into high shouting pillars of foam. The roar and thunder of the guns, the scream of approaching shells, the harsh clang as steel splinters struck home and the smell of burnt cordite, all these combined in the blinding moment of battle. Aboard the Prince of Wales, while the cry of shells drew nearer and nearer, they waited anxiously to see at which ship the Bismarck was firing. A second later, as a forest of foam leapt up ahead of the Hood, they knew that the Germans were concentrating on the leading ship.

A second salvo fell astern of the Hood. The collapsing spray added to the difficulties of the gunnery officer and range takers in the Prince of Wales. The high speed at which the two ships had gone into action had blinded the range finders of the forward turrets with spray. Fire had been opened on the range obtained from the small range finder of the control position. (It is possible that the Hood also opened fire on ranges obtained from her control range finder.)

On the horizon the Norfolk and Suffolk watched and waited. Two signalmen on the Norfolk's bridge kept their telescopes trained all the time upon the Hood. They saw the brown clouds of cordite smoke lift as her forward guns opened fire. They saw the white pillars spring out of the sea around her as the Bismarck replied. It seemed to them that the Hood's first two salvos were close to the enemy, and a third salvo seemed to straddle her.

Suddenly, as the Bismarck's third salvo fell, a great glow of fire sprang up close to the Hood's mainmast. It wavered and pulsated—a huge, orange ball of flame with little smoke to it. The Hood had been hit!

The time was now 5:55 A.M. The watchers on the bridge of the Prince of Wales saw that the Admiral had made another signal—a turn by blue pendant—20 degrees to port together. The turn would have brought the two ships round on to an almost parallel course with the Bismarck. It would have opened the "A" arcs of both ships, and would have allowed the full weight of their salvos to be brought to bear. Just as the pendant dropped from the Hood's yardarm a fourth salvo from the Bismarck fell close to her. Both the British ships began to execute the turn.

Admiral Lutjens had been concentrating the fire of his two ships upon the Hood. He had recognized her silhouette from the moment that the action had been joined, but he was still under the misapprehension that the Prince of Wales was her sister ship, the King George V.* He realized now that he had been brought to bay by two of the heaviest ships in the British fleet. But he could at least congratulate himself on the fact that the Bismarck's firing was excellent. It looked as if he had straddled the Hood with his second salvo, and his third appeared to have hit. He could see a great fire raging on the British battle cruiser's boat-deck, even as the fifth salvo left his guns.

The fifth salvo, hurtling through the air, was history. The Hood and the Prince of Wales were swinging fast to port and their "A" arcs were just opening. From one of the Hood's after-turrets a salvo had just fired. Then the great flame and the high sobbing scream burst. At a range of 16,500 yards the Hood had received her death blow. A pillar of fire soared into the air—a thousand feet high. Guns and turrets were plucked from their mountings and tossed aside like toys. Masts collapsed, hundreds of tons of steel rained on to the water, and the northern sky was split by thunder. She heeled to port. Her back broke. Her bows and stern lifted like two giant tombstones to her dead.

*In all the German signals the Prince of Wales was referred to as the King George V.

Captain Leach, following close astern, had to alter course to avoid the wreckage. As the Prince of Wales came abreast the Hood's fast-disappearing bows, the water was up to "A" turret. The bows lifted to an angle of 45 degrees and then slid back with a great sigh into the sea. There was nothing left now but a dense column of smoke towering over the scarred water. She had sunk within two minutes.

The Hood's grave is in 63° 21′ N., 31° 50′ W. If ever a ship died in action, the Hood did. Her last salvo was in the air at the moment when she received the final blow. Every man was at his post; the breeches had just slammed behind shells and charges for a further salvo; she was steaming still at 28 knots; and then the night and darkness covered her. One minute she was alive, the next minute dead.

She lies deep in the waters of the north, washed by the cold currents of the Denmark Strait, five hundred miles northeast of Cape Farewell.

23

Revenge

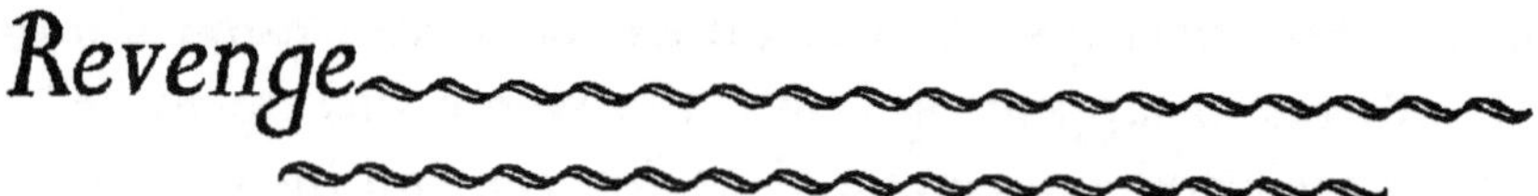

The loss was broadcast at 9 P.M. on May 24. The Admiralty communiqué read:

> British naval forces intercepted early this morning off the coast of Greenland German naval forces including the battleship Bismarck.
>
> The enemy were attacked and during the ensuing action H.M.S. Hood (Captain R. Kerr, C.B.E., R.N.) wearing the flag of Vice-Admiral L. E. Holland, C.B., received an unlucky hit in the magazine and blew up.
>
> The Bismarck has received damage and the pursuit of the enemy continues.
>
> It is feared there will be few survivors from H.M.S. Hood.

The effect of the news was out of all proportion to the loss of one ship, however large and important she might have been.* Coming as it did, hard on the heels of the German successes in Crete, the news seemed little less than a national disaster. It was not only the fleet which mourned the Hood. For so many years,

*At the time, the author was serving in H.M.S. Glenroy. The ship had just returned to Alexandria after an ineffectual attempt to land reinforcements in Crete. I remember with what tragic force the news of the Hood's loss struck us. Our senior quartermaster, "Lofty" Earl (later to be lost in the Breconshire), who had served his boy's time aboard the Hood, broke down on hearing the news.

she had represented to millions of people the whole spirit of the Royal Navy. For so long, she had been not only the largest ship in the fleet, but in the world. Her size, coupled with her dignified and graceful lines, had made her in many people's minds the very essence and symbol of the great warship.

Ninety-four officers and 1,321 ratings were lost in that brief moment. There were only three survivors*—Midshipman W. J. Dundas, Able Seaman R. E. Tilburn, and Ordinary Signalman A. E. Briggs. They were picked up by the destroyers, who had been sweeping thirty miles away at the time of the action. Recalled by Rear-Admiral Wake-Walker, the destroyers found no more than these three men and a little floating wreckage. The scent of cordite, fuel oil, and disaster hung over the gray sea.

Admiral Wake-Walker in the Norfolk now found himself the senior officer. But the situation had changed drastically in those five minutes. At 5:55 A.M. the Rear-Admiral had been watching from the sidelines. The main task of his two cruisers had been successfully accomplished from the moment that the two British heavy units appeared on the scene. At 6 A.M. the Hood had sunk. The Bismarck had rapidly shifted target to the Prince of Wales, and the latter was clearly in a bad way. The range had closed to about 18,000 yards when, at 6:02 A.M., a 15-inch shell struck her compass platform, killing or wounding every man there, with the exception of the captain. Hit by four 15-inch shells from the Bismarck, as well as by a number of 8-inch from the Prinz Eugen, the Prince of Wales hauled away under cover of smoke.

*While writing this book, I heard a rumor that there had been a fourth survivor from H.M.S. Hood. The facts are as follows, and are borne out by reports in the *Daily Express* (July 9, 1942), and the *News Chronicle* (August 16, 1942): A man charged at West London Police Court with being in the possession of a false identity card stated that he had been a stoker in the Hood, had been picked up by a trawler, and landed at Liverpool. He had not reported back to the Navy.

On investigation, it proved that he was a deserter from the R.A.S.C., and that it was his brother who had been lost in the Hood. He was sentenced to three months' imprisonment for possessing a false identity card, and for assuming a false name.

Throughout this brief action, the German gunnery had been of the first order. The Bismarck had opened fire with deadly accuracy on the Hood, straddling and hitting her with the third salvo; just as in World War I the Germans had proved that their gunnery control and their range finders were second to none. With the Hood gone, the defects in the Prince of Wales as a fighting machine quickly became apparent. One gun in a forward turret had become defective from the first salvo; one turret was now out of action; her bridge was wrecked; and she had sustained damage aft. It was a disastrous situation. But, although Rear-Admiral Wake-Walker could not know it at that moment, the last salvos fired by the Prince of Wales had resulted in three hits on the Bismarck. One of these, in a port oil-bunker, was to cause a serious loss of fuel as well as contamination of the battleship's fuel-supply system. The Bismarck also had one boiler room flooded, and her speed was reduced. The effect of the damage caused Admiral Lutjens to abandon his raid into the Atlantic.

In view of the condition of the Prince of Wales, Admiral Wake-Walker decided to keep the battleship with him as part of the shadowing force. But he would not attempt to engage the enemy until he had been reinforced. He knew that Sir John Tovey in the King George V was still some 330 miles to the southward of him, and that the Commander-in-Chief had with him the aircraft carrier Victorious, as well as four cruisers and nine destroyers. So long as Admiral Wake-Walker continued to keep in touch with the Bismarck, he would once again be able to bring other heavy units to battle with her. The Admiralty, meanwhile, had detached the Rodney, and the old battleship Ramillies, from their respective convoys and ordered them to close the area.

Admiral Lutjens could congratulate himself on the immediate success of the action. He had sunk the Hood, and had driven off the Prince of Wales. But the damage inflicted on his own vessel had ruined his chances for carrying out operation RHEINUEBUNG. While the Bismarck made her way to Brest for repairs, he decided to detach the Prinz Eugen. Heavy rain sweeping up from the Atlantic made the diversion somewhat easier. While proceeding on a mean course of southwest, he continued to make a number of large-scale alterations of course, under cover of the driving squalls. During one of these alterations he managed to detach the Prinz Eugen successfully. She slipped away toward the south, as the Bismarck kept the shadowing cruisers at bay.

The operations which followed are classic in naval history. They involve immense problems of search and co-operation. One of the most complex problems was the fuel range of widely varying classes of ships. The situation was met by the Admiralty with a confidence and efficiency which cannot be too highly praised. If the loss of the Hood had shaken people's faith in British ship design, the pursuit and destruction of the Bismarck showed that the overall control of the naval war was in competent hands.

At 1:20 P.M. the shadowing cruisers reported to Admiral Tovey that the enemy had altered course to the south, and had reduced speed to 24 knots. A Sunderland flying boat had previously reported that the battleship was leaving a long oil slick behind her, a fact which the Suffolk had also confirmed.

The Commander-in-Chief could now be fairly confident that the enemy was damaged (although how badly he could not know), and was most probably making for the Atlantic coast of France. On the previous night, the Admiralty had ordered Admiral Somerville and Force H to leave Gibraltar and proceed to the north to cover the approaches to the Bay of Biscay. Admiral Tovey realized that unless the Bismarck's speed was further reduced, there was every chance of her making good her escape before he could engage, or before Force H could successfully block the enemy's retreat. Accordingly, at 3 P.M. he detached the aircraft carrier Victorious and the Second Cruiser Squadron to proceed to a position about 100 miles from the enemy, and to fly off a torpedo-bomber attack.

Led by Lieutenant-Commander E. Esmonde, nine Swordfish escorted by five Fulmars took off at 10 P.M. The weather was bad for flying operations, and a heavy sea and driving rain made location of the target difficult. The squadron's first radar contact, which brought them down below the cloud base ready for attack, proved to be the Norfolk. Once again the shadowing cruiser fulfilled her traditional role in homing the attacking force on to the enemy. It was shortly after this that the U.S. Coast Guard cutter, Modoc, peacefully keeping her Atlantic station, found herself involved in the hunt for the Bismarck. The Swordfish picked up the ship by radar (she was on the same bearing as the Bismarck) and swept out of the cloud ready to attack. Although the Modoc did not know it, she was in the center of the most dramatic ship hunt of the war. Aircraft and warships were converging on all sides of her.

The squadron's third radar contact proved to be the right one. A few minutes after midnight, eight of the Swordfish* pressed home their attack against heavy and accurate gunfire. The Bismarck was steaming hard to the southwest, her powerful hull and superstructure outlined against the declining sun. One attack, carried home with great gallantry by Lieutenant P. Gick, R.N., resulted in a hit on the starboard side amidships, just below the Bismarck's aircraft catapult.

The hit caused little serious damage to a ship of Bismarck's strength, although it led to her first casualty, Leading Seaman Kirchberg. (The three shells from the Prince of Wales had inflicted serious damage, but had caused no loss of life.) For the first time almost, the German sailors realized that they would not be allowed to get away with their success of the morning.

*One Swordfish had lost contact with the squadron. All of them subsequently regained the Victorious, although two Fulmars were lost.

Admiral Lutjens was now aware that the British radar would not permit him to shake off pursuit as easily as he had hoped. It was radar which had held him through the Denmark Strait, and it was radar which had enabled the Swordfish to carry out their torpedo strike. He had successfully launched the Prinz Eugen on her foray into the Atlantic, but the fate of his own ship was still uncertain.

While the congratulatory messages poured in from Germany, and while millions of allies still mourned the loss of the Hood, the Bismarck's Admiral was worried. It was easy for his *Fuehrer* to say "You are the pride of the Navy," but Admiral Lutjens could sense the net closing about him. The bitter irony was that if he had never engaged the Hood and the Prince of Wales and had turned for home, RHEINUEBUNG would only have been postponed. In his very success lay the seed of his failure.

At 4 A.M. on the twenty-fifth the Suffolk lost contact with the Bismarck. Two hours later, after she and the Norfolk had further searched the area, the Commander-in-Chief received the news.* The King George V at that moment was little more than 100 miles away from the enemy's position. Admiral Tovey's feelings can be imagined, as he realized that his hopes of bringing the Bismarck to action in the next few hours were doomed. The only man who would have welcomed the news seems to have been unaware of what had happened. Admiral Lutjens, convinced by now of the efficiency of British radar, felt that wireless silence was unimportant. He continued to send out wireless transmissions to the German Admiralty.

Throughout the day that followed, these transmissions were picked up by the Admiralty in London. Owing to a mistake in the plotting of the bearings, it was first of all assumed that the enemy was heading back for the North Sea via the Iceland–Faeroes channel. Admiral Tovey immediately reversed his course

*Under extremely unfavorable conditions, the cruisers had held the enemy for nearly thirty-two hours.

to northeast, and adjusted the movements of the other ships under his command to cover this new eventuality. It was not until 3:30 P.M. on the twenty-fifth that the Admiralty gave it as their opinion that the enemy had not altered course, and that he was still heading in the same direction. At 6:05 P.M. they instructed the Rodney to cover the line of retreat toward Brest. At almost the same moment Admiral Tovey altered back to the southeast. Unfortunately, the confusion caused by the wrong estimation of the enemy's intentions had made him fall farther astern of the Bismarck, so that he was now about 150 miles behind her. Force H, meanwhile, was still steaming hard to the north, having been directed earlier in the day to assume that the Bismarck was making for Brest. The battleship Rodney (Captain Dalrymple-Hamilton) had come to this conclusion from the beginning. She, too, was laying herself across the Bismarck's path.

The long night of the twenty-fifth wore on. It was over thirty-six hours since the Hood had sunk, and it was many hours since contact with the Bismarck had been lost. A rising sea and a cold wind from the northwest made the search more difficult, and the bitterness of the men engaged in it more acute. It was unthinkable that their comrades should go unavenged, and—on a sterner basis—it was unthinkable that the Bismarck should escape them, perhaps to refuel from a tanker deep in the Atlantic and carry out her warfare against merchant shipping. The glass went on falling, and the wind in the Bay of Biscay was rapidly rising to gale force as Force H labored northward. Just as on the occasion of his breakout from Bergen, the weather remained in Admiral Lutjens' favor.

At 10:30 A.M. on May 26 the confusions of the past twenty-four hours were finally resolved. A Catalina flying boat of Coastal Command, piloted by Pilot Officer D. A. Briggs, sighted the Bismarck.

> [We were] at 500 feet when we saw a warship. I was in the second's pilot's seat when the occupant of the seat beside me,

> an American, said: "What the devil's that?" I stared and saw a dull black shape through the mist which curled above a very rough sea. "Looks like a battleship," he said. I said: "Better get closer. Go round its stern."*

The Bismarck immediately opened fire, and the Catalina was hit in several places. Fortunately there were no casualties, and the aircraft's sighting report was sent off. Less than three-quarters of an hour later the Bismarck was again sighted. This time it was by a Swordfish, one of an air search of ten planes which had been flown off by the Ark Royal, who was some seventy miles to the eastward.

The pursuit of the Bismarck from the moment that she left Norway is an interesting example of the co-operation of various services, and various methods. She had been sighted first by a Coastal Command reconnaissance aircraft. Her absence from Bergen had been reported by the Fleet Air Arm. She was then sighted visually by Able Seaman Newell. She was held and shadowed by radar. Lost in the snowstorms of the Denmark Strait, she was found again by radar. After the destruction of the Hood, she was held by visual and radar shadowing. Lost a second time, she was rediscovered by an R.A.F. flying boat. Final contact was made by the Ark Royal's Swordfish.

Although Sir John Tovey now had news of the enemy, he had little reason to be cheerful. The Bismarck was a long way to the southeast of his flagship, and before very long would come within the German air umbrella operating from France. How many U-boats might have been sent out to cover her withdrawal, and to lie in wait for his own forces, he could not know. Unless the Bismarck were slowed down even further, there was every chance that at a speed of 20 knots or more, she would be under cover from her own forces shortly after dawn on the twenty-seventh. The problem of fuel shortage in both the Rodney and the King George V added to the Admiral's worries. The Renown was too lightly armored to be able to engage the Bismarck with any

**Coastal Command* (London, His Majesty's Stationery Office, 1942).

chances of success. It seemed that nothing short of a successful torpedo attack by the Ark Royal's aircraft, or by the Fourth Destroyer Flotilla, could prevent the enemy from winning to safety.

The Fourth Destroyer Flotilla, under Captain P. L. Vian, D.S.O., had been on Atlantic convoy duty. The five destroyers Cossack, Maori, Sikh, Zulu, and the Polish Piorun* had been steaming to meet the Commander-in-Chief, when the news of the Catalina sighting came through. Although he had been ordered to join Sir John Tovey to screen the flagship, Captain Vian decided that the more urgent task was to find and, if possible, attack the Bismarck. He altered course accordingly to close the enemy's reported position, and increased to full speed.

At 2:50 P.M. on May 26 the first of the Ark Royal's torpedo striking force was flown off. It consisted of fourteen Swordfish. Weather conditions were appalling, low gray scud covering the horizon, and the flightdeck of the carrier rising and falling like a monstrous elevator. The aircraft had been flying for about half an hour when a radar contact was reported. Instantly the planes came down through the cloud and turned for the target. Almost at the very moment they released their torpedoes, they realized their mistake. The ship ahead of them, laboring through the heavy seas, was not the German battleship, but the cruiser Sheffield—some twenty miles to the north of their target.

Captain Larcom of the Sheffield, who had been expecting to sight the aircraft and to con them on to the Bismarck, saw to his dismay that his own ship had become the target. He rang down for full speed, ordered his guns not to fire, and just managed to evade the torpedoes.

The news that the Ark Royal's first strike had been a complete failure added to the gloom in the British ships. Dusk would soon be falling over the lumpy wind-swept waters of the Atlantic. With every minute that passed, it seemed as if the Bismarck was

*The Poles had a personal score to settle. Four midshipmen of the Polish Navy had gone down in the Hood.

certain to make good her escape. Sir John Tovey realized that there was probably only time for one more attempt to be made by the Ark's aircraft that day. His own flagship and the Rodney were both short of fuel, and the latter had reported that she could not remain after 8 A.M. on the following morning. Short of a successful strike by the Ark Royal's next flight, or a lucky torpedo attack by Captain Vian's destroyers, the situation seemed almost hopeless. He knew, too, that a battleship of the Bismarck's caliber was likely to be able to withstand a number of torpedoes without being appreciably slowed down.

On the previous day Admiral Lutjens had addressed the crew of the Bismarck. "We did not intend to fight enemy warships," he had said, "but to wage war against merchant shipping. Through treachery the enemy managed to find us in the Denmark Strait. We took up the fight. The crew have behaved magnificently. We shall win or die."*

At 7:15 P.M. the second wave of fifteen Swordfish left the Ark Royal. Lieutenant-Commander T. P. Coode was the strike leader. This time the instructions were clear—the aircraft would first of all find the Sheffield (who was still following about twelve miles astern of the Bismarck), and would proceed from her in a coordinated attack on the battleship. Less than an hour before the aircraft took off, Sir John Tovey had been compelled to make the bitter signal that—unless the enemy's speed had been reduced before midnight—he would be compelled to turn back and refuel. The situation was increasingly desperate. He had been hard on the Bismarck's heels for over 2,000 miles. The Hood was still unavenged. The last Swordfish strike by the Ark Royal had been fruitless. By morning the enemy would be secure.

Rainstorms swept the sea, and the cloud base was down to 2,000 feet, when the aircraft passed over the Sheffield to learn the Bismarck's bearing and distance from her. The cruiser re-

*Martiennsen, *Hitler and His Admirals.*

ported that the enemy was twelve miles dead ahead. The Swordfish bucketing in the strong winds headed toward their target. Their attacks were spread over a period of half an hour, and all of them came under the German battleship's usual accurate fire. Although she had been damaged in the course of the long action, both her main and secondary armament were still in full fighting efficiency.

The Fleet Air Arm, which had been first with the news that the Bismarck was out, was also responsible for the blow that finally crippled her.

". . . Aircraft approached us from all sides," wrote Ordinary Seaman Manthey of the Bismarck.* "I do not know the exact number. I felt two heavy shakings of the ship, one shortly after the other. The attacks were dive-bombing attacks, coming from the clouds to about ten to twenty meters above the water. We thought the attacks were made very pluckily."

At 9:05 P.M. Admiral Lutjens signaled, "Torpedo hit aft," and at 9:15 P.M., "Torpedo hit amidships." It was the hit aft which decided the fate of the great battleship. The 18-inch aircraft torpedo amidships did little harm to the Bismarck's heavy armor belt, but the hit aft found her Achilles' heel. It exploded in the ship's steering compartment, and jammed the rudder hard to starboard.

Over the Bismarck's loud-speaker system the announcement went out. "Rudder jammed hard a-starboard." Divers went down into the flooded compartment, and set to work on coupling up the hand-steering system. As the night came down over the sea and the crippled giant strove to regain control, telegrams of congratulations for the sinking of the Hood were still pouring in. By order of the *Fuehrer*, Lieutenant-Commander Schneider was awarded the Knight's Cross of the Iron Cross for his part in the action against the British battle cruiser. It was Admiral Lutjens' birthday. He, too, received a special message from Adolf Hitler:

*Martiennsen, *Hitler and His Admirals.*

"... The whole of Germany is with you." Aircraft were promised for the next day, and the crew were told that two tugs, a tanker, and U-boats were on their way to help them.

That night Captain Vian's destroyers came in against her. The sky was brilliant with the glow of star shells as they made their attacks. The Bismarck's shooting was still excellent. Damaged though she was, and with a full gale blowing, she opened rapid fire on the mosquitolike ships that leapt toward her through the heavy seas. Admiral Tovey meanwhile was steering westward to get into position for a dawn attack. His intention was to have the German battleship silhouetted against the light of the rising sun. By now, there were so many British ships closing the scene, as well as in contact with the enemy, that he had decided against the risks involved in a night action.

It is not known for certain what hits, if any, were scored by Captain Vian's ships during the tumult of those dark hours. Survivors from the Bismarck stated that no torpedoes struck them, but their evidence is little more reliable than that of the British destroyers. In the thunder of a gale, with main and secondary armament firing, it would be difficult for battle-tired men to know whether they had in fact been hit by a torpedo—unless they were in the immediate vicinity. On the other hand, the conditions under which the destroyer attacks were pressed home were such that it was almost impossible for their captains or their torpedo control officers to be sure of results. The brilliant flash of the Bismarck's guns replying to the destroyer attacks may well have been taken as the explosions of torpedoes striking home.

The dawn came slowly over the bitter sea. As the Bismarck wallowed erratically now west, now north of west (she had long since been unable to pursue her course toward the southeast and safety) the destroyers settled grimly on her flanks. They waited while the avengers crept over the horizon. A few minutes before 9 A.M. Sir John Tovey in the King George V and Captain Dalrymple-Hamilton in the Rodney sighted the German battleship. She was almost twelve miles ahead of them. They at once brought to bear on her the weight of their 14-inch and 16-inch guns. The Rodney was the first to open fire, just as she was the first to be fired at by the indomitable enemy.*

The end of the Bismarck came slowly. There was no hope for her. "As the hits increased, the antiaircraft crews went under cover. We had the impression that we were fired on from all sides." By 10:15 A.M. the giant hull had become a shambles of tortured metal, bulkheads glowing with internal fires, and the roar of exploding shells and ammunition drowning the eternal rumor of the sea.

The Rodney and the King George V were now at ranges of about 9,000 yards—point-blank for their heavy guns. The German battleship had become little more than a practice target for their salvos. At 10:20 A.M. the cruiser Dorsetshire, who had arrived on the scene an hour before, closed the stricken ship to administer the death blow. As one of the Dorsetshire's officers later wrote:†

> She was a terrible sight. Her top was blown clear away, flames were roaring out in several places, and her plates were glowing red with heat. Great clouds of black smoke were billowing from her and rising for several hundred feet or so.
>
> It was the end.
>
> We asked permission to finish her off with torpedoes. We fired, hitting her abreast of the bridge. The Bismarck settled down by the stern, and then heeled over to port. She had not blown up, but just went straight down on her side with her battle ensign flying. It was a most impressive sight, and we watched in silence as she finally went under.

It was 10:36 A.M. on May 27 when the Bismarck rolled her bilges to the sky and sank. She lies in 48° 10′ N., 16° 12′ W.,

*One or two newspapers at the time referred to the demoralization of the Bismarck's crew in the last stages of the action. I well remember with what sick disgust a shipmate showed me one of these reports. Like all of us in the fleet, he had nothing but admiration and respect for the outstanding gallantry with which the Bismarck had fought.

†Ministry of Information.

many miles from her great adversary, but claimed in the end by the same ocean. The Hood and the Bismarck had been the two greatest warships of their respective eras, and they were the only ship casualties in the whole of the operation.

Covered by the same ocean, they lie deep. The long Atlantic swell will never stir their hulls. Until all the seas run dry, they have no memorial except in the minds of men.

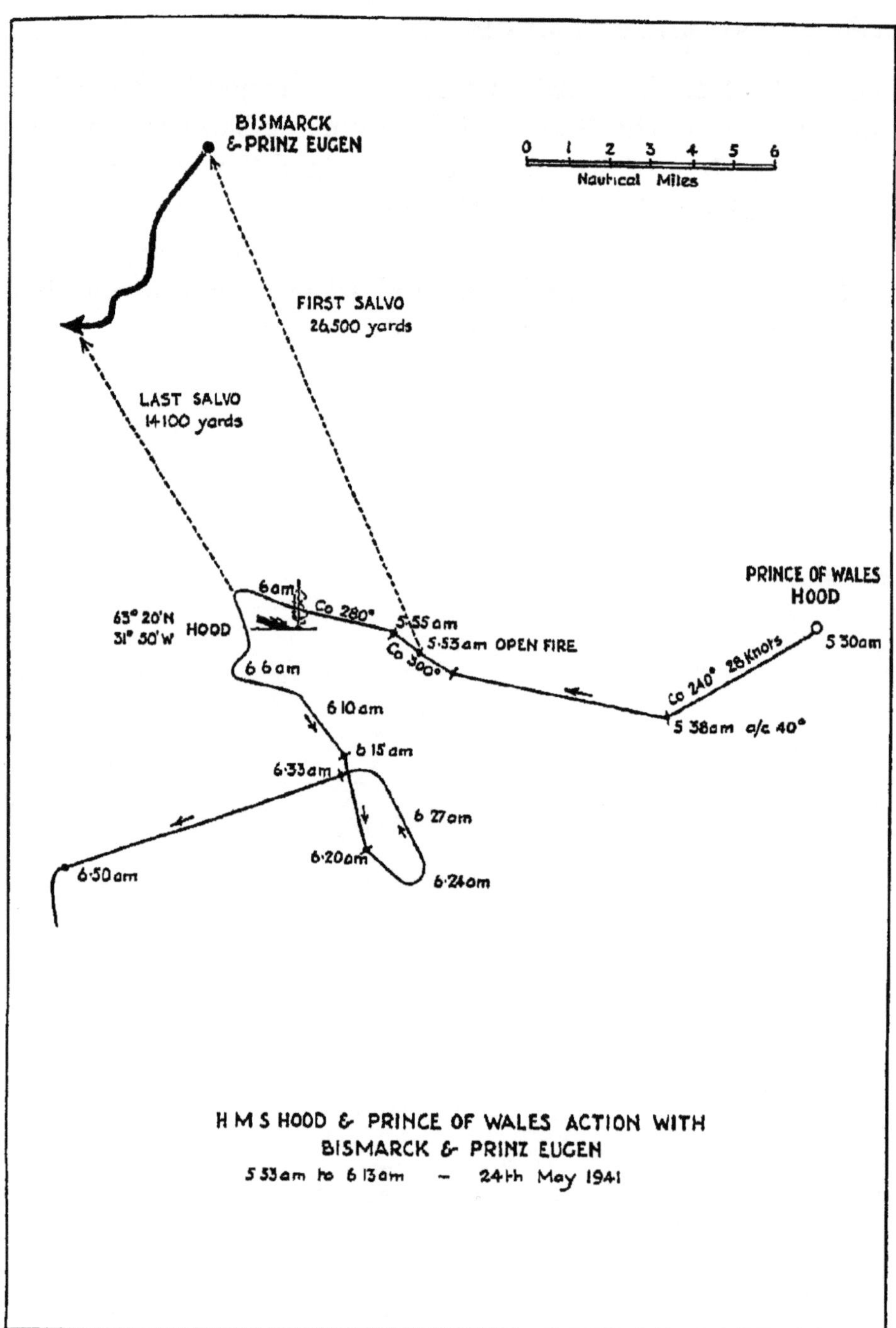

H M S HOOD & PRINCE OF WALES ACTION WITH
BISMARCK & PRINZ EUGEN
5 53am to 6 13am – 24th May 1941

24

Post-Mortem

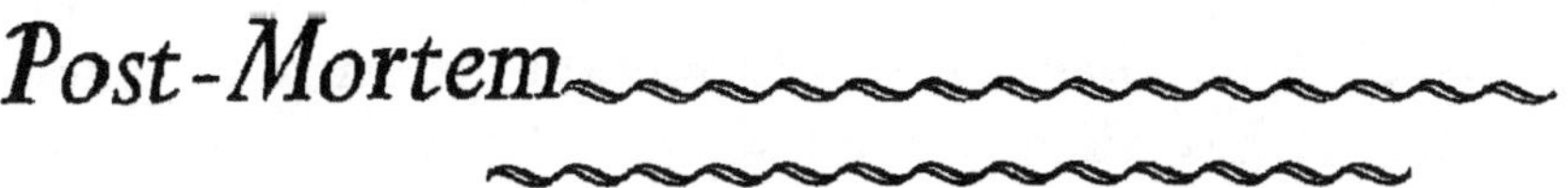

To discover what really happened in the Hood's last battle, and how it was that her end was so sudden and violent, recalling the British battle cruiser losses at Jutland, one must go back to 5:35 A.M. It was at that moment that the British squadron sighted the German ships and made their final approach.

The Hood and the Prince of Wales were steering a course of 240 degrees at a speed of 28 knots. At 5:38 A.M. they altered course 40 degrees to starboard, bringing them to a true course of 280 degrees. As we have seen, Admiral Holland's alterations during the night of May 23/24 had caused him to lose bearing on the enemy. On the morning of the twenty-fourth, therefore, he was never able to make an ideal interception from a position ahead of the Bismarck and Prinz Eugen. When the ships came into action at 5:52 A.M., the Hood and the Prince of Wales were steering 300 degrees. The Bismarck was fine on their starboard bow, so that they were unable to bring their after-turrets to bear, and were thus at a great disadvantage. From the German point of view the British ships were slightly forward of their beam. The Bismarck and the Prinz Eugen could bring the full weight of their salvos to bear (eight 15-inch and eight 8-inch). The Hood and the Prince of Wales had lost the advantage of their greater firepower.

At this stage of the battle it would seem clear that Admiral Holland's main objective was to shorten the range as quickly as possible. It has already been suggested that it was the known weakness of his flagship which may have caused him to decide on a battle at close quarters. It has also been pointed out that the Prince of Wales was deficient in training, and that her turrets were known to be suffering from teething troubles. There was every reason, then, why the Admiral should decide to fight a comparatively close engagement, especially when one takes into consideration the known caliber of his opponent, and the fact that it might be assumed that the Bismarck was 100 per cent worked up and battleworthy.

It has been asked, why was the Prince of Wales not placed in the van? The Admiral knew that her deck armor was heavier than the Hood's, and that she might be expected to be capable of taking more punishment during the opening phase of the battle than the older ship. One good reason would seem to be the known defect of the Prince of Wales' forward turrets, whereby one of the guns would become inoperative immediately after the first salvo was fired.* A second reason why Admiral Holland may have preferred to lead was that it might be assumed the Hood's gunnery would be more efficient than that of the less-trained Prince of Wales. In conclusion, it would appear that the Admiral was prepared to accept the disadvantages of an approach with "A" arcs closed, in the initial stages of the battle in order to close the range. He had just reached the point at which his two ships were being turned parallel to the Germans—and when the "A" arcs were opening—when the Hood was blown up.

It has been suggested that uppermost in Admiral Holland's

*In the event, the two British ships, from the first salvo onward, were bringing to bear only four 15-inch (the Hood's forward turrets) and five 14-inch (the Prince of Wales' forward turrets less one gun).

mind was the necessity for closing range, in which case a steep angle of approach toward the enemy was inevitable. What does not seem so clear is why the squadron's angle of approach was not even steeper than it was. To gain the maximum advantage, the Hood and the Prince of Wales should have approached the enemy bows-on. In fact, when they opened fire at 5:52 A.M. the Bismarck was bearing Green 30, thirty degrees on the Hood's starboard bow. The British squadron thus had the worst of both worlds. They could not bring their broadsides to bear, neither were they presenting to the enemy the minimum lateral target. It is known that the Commander-in-Chief, Admiral Sir John Tovey, favored an end-on approach during the initial stages of an action. Admiral Holland, therefore, most probably had this in mind when bringing his ships to battle. Unfortunately, he seems to have adopted a compromise. His ships were not presenting only their beam to the enemy (as would have been the case with a true end-on approach), but, by steering about 30 degrees to port of an end-on course, nearly half of his ships were presented as a target.

The two British ships were maneuvered into battle in close order—800 yards apart. Without any doubt it seems that this was a mistake. Although it was the conventional and accepted method, as laid down in Admiralty Fighting Instructions, the close-order formation could have had no possible advantage for the Hood and the Prince of Wales. In theory, two heavy ships maneuvering as one unit in close order should be able to bring the maximum of their firepower to bear, the two ships becoming, as it were, one fighting machine. If the two ships had been of similar class, and therefore identical in all respects, there might have been something to be said for close order. But the Hood and the Prince of Wales were completely different types of vessel, with different armor, armament, and speeds. The close-order formation, in fact, gave the Bismarck the chance to shift her fire on to the Prince of Wales within a few seconds of the Hood being sunk. Had the Prince of Wales been at open order (one thousand yards) or, better still, a mile distant from the Hood, she would have had more freedom to maneuver. The German gunners would also have had more difficulty in ranging on their second target.

In the earlier stages of the approach, it may have seemed wise to Admiral Holland to maintain a policy of radar silence. (He wished to give the Germans no possible chance of suspecting that British heavy units were on their way to cut them off.) He had also made the signal that radar should not be used until action was imminent. Fire was in fact opened on optical range-finder ranges, and the Prince of Wales obtained no radar ranges from either her gunnery or her search radar set throughout the action. It may reasonably be assumed that the Hood was in a similar case. As radar was in its infancy in those days it is possible that in any case radar ranges would have been disregarded in favor of optical ranges. It would seem, though, that had the British radar sets been tuned up and working for some time before the Bismarck and Prinz Eugen were sighted, radar ranges more accurate than those obtained by the optical range finders would have improved the British gunnery.*

The last question which remains to be considered is, at which ship was the Hood firing during the brief eight minutes of the action? At 5:49 A.M. Admiral Holland had signaled for a concentration of fire on the leading ship, and we have seen how this mistake in identification had arisen. The Prince of Wales had all along come to the conclusion that the Bismarck was the right-hand ship, and had decided to ignore the Admiral's order. At 5:52 A.M., however, at the very moment of opening fire, the Admiral realized his mistake and signaled for a shift of target on to the Bismarck. What will never be known with any certainty is

*Especially when it is borne in mind that the spray sweeping the ships was blinding the range finders of their forward turrets. The Prince of Wales was also at a disadvantage from the Hood's smoke obscuring the range.

whether this shift of target ever became known to the Hood's main armament control.

A German account of the action states that the Prinz Eugen came under fire from the heavy artillery, and one can only assume that these shells were fired by the Hood. There is no doubt that, from the beginning of the action, the Prince of Wales was firing at the Bismarck. No other ships were engaged, although it is true that the Suffolk from her position astern of the Bismarck did fire a few salvos. These fell a long way short, and even if they had fallen close to the Prinz Eugen, they could never have been confused with 15-inch shells.

Admiral Lutjens, in his signal to the German Admiralty, stated that his ship had come under concentrated fire from the Hood. The hits received by the Bismarck he ascribed, though, to "the King George."* The two cruisers, Norfolk and Suffolk, thought that the Hood was firing accurately at the Bismarck—but the cruisers were some ten to fourteen miles away from the enemy. At that range it would be difficult, if not impossible, to distinguish between the fall of shot from the Hood and that from the Prince of Wales. The real truth of the matter will never be known.

The fact that Admiral Lutjens ascribed the hits received by his ship to the Prince of Wales suggests that she was hit after the Hood was sunk—otherwise how could he have been sure? In the opinion of Ordinary Seaman Mantney, one of the Bismarck's survivors, ". . . these three hits were caused by the last enemy cruiser [battleship]."

In the roar and confusion of battle, when one's own guns are firing and enemy shells are falling all around, even the coolest and most logical of men is liable to mistakes. One would like to think that it was the Hood's last salvo—the salvo which she fired almost at the moment of her disintegration—which damaged the Bismarck and reduced her speed. But real life cannot be dis-

*The Prince of Wales. See footnote, page 193.

torted to suit the terms of fiction. The loss of Admiral Holland, and later of Admiral Lutjens, removed from the scene the only two witnesses upon whose evidence the truth of the Hood's last action could be properly assessed.

What caused the Hood to sink so quickly? The evidence of the watchers in the two cruisers, of the Hood's three survivors, and of the officers in the Prince of Wales must all be considered. The evidence of the cruiser Norfolk, who was about 20,000 yards from the Hood during the action, is as reliable as any. Since the Hood was the senior officer's ship, two signalmen on the bridge of the Norfolk had their telescopes trained all the time on the battle cruiser to watch for any signals she might make.

The ships opened fire in the following order—Hood, Bismarck, and Prince of Wales. The opening salvo from the Bismarck fell ahead of the Hood. Her second salvo fell between the Hood and the Prince of Wales. The third appeared to straddle the Hood. It was after this third salvo that the fire was seen on Hood's boat-deck. It is most likely that out of this salvo, one shell, at least, hit the Hood. The Bismarck's fourth salvo fell just over, astern of Hood, and her fifth seemed to straddle and hit. It was with the Bismarck's fifth salvo, at a gun range of 16,500 yards, that the Hood blew up.

Captain Phillips of the Norfolk, who had been a former gunnery officer aboard the Hood and therefore knew the ship well, associated the fire arising from the Bismarck's third salvo as being due to a hit on the Hood's upperdeck torpedo tubes. Had the upperdeck torpedo tubes gone up, however, what would have been seen by the observers would have been a shattering explosion—not a great, glowing fire.

Able Seaman R. E. Tilburn was the only survivor from the Hood who was in a position to see aft during the action. (Ordinary Signalman A. E. Briggs was on the compass platform, and Midshipman W. J. Dundas was on the closed upper bridge, which had no view aft.) Tilburn's opinion was that the hit from the Bismarck's third salvo was on the boatdeck, in the vicinity of the port midship U.P. mounting. A fierce fire immediately started, and some of the ready-use 4-inch ammunition, which was stowed nearby, began to explode. A hit by a 15-inch shell would undoubtedly have set off not only the 4-inch ready-use ammunition, but also the U.P. ammunition. This was stowed in light metal lockers on the boatdeck.*

The concensus of opinion seems to have been that the fire on the Hood's boatdeck was in the nature of a cordite fire. It was not a sudden explosion. Four-inch ammunition and U.P. ammunition would have produced the effect of a glowing fire "that seemed to pulsate."

The evidence of the Prince of Wales agrees that the fire started on Hood's boatdeck with the Bismarck's third salvo, and that it was a reddish or orange wavering fire. Captain Leach described it as "like a vast blow-lamp," and the second gunnery officer of the Prince of Wales said that the smoke was dark yellow in color. All this would seem to agree with the description of its being a cordite fire.

A hit on the Hood's boatdeck setting off the ready-use ammunition would not have caused the loss of the ship. According to Midshipman Dundas, the Hood's torpedo officer, who was standing at the starboard after-end of the bridge, reported a cordite fire on the starboard side of the boatdeck after the fall of the Bismarck's third salvo. This is confirmed by Signalman Briggs, who heard the Hood's senior gunnery officer report to Vice-Admiral Holland, "Hit on boatdeck and fire in ready-use locker." The Admiral's reply to this (and his last recorded words) was: "Leave it until the ammunition is gone."

The final conclusion would seem to be that the Bismarck hit the Hood with her third salvo, but that this hit which started a

*See page 124. The unrotated-projectile equipment never proved effective against aircraft. Not long after the loss of the Hood, its use was discontinued throughout the fleet, and the equipment was removed.

fire on the battle cruiser's boatdeck was not responsible for her death. It was the hit, or hits, from the fifth salvo, that destroyed the ship. The fire from the first hit was still burning when the ship blew up.

There is a general agreement from all the watchers that the Bismarck's fifth salvo not only straddled the Hood, but hit her. The exact position of the hit would seem to have been in the same locality as the previous one—on the boatdeck, somewhere near the mainmast. It is possible that more than one shell from this fifth salvo hit the Hood, and that the position on which a second 15-inch shell struck home could not be seen by the watchers in the cruisers or the Prince of Wales. This hit, or hits, caused a large explosion but, strangely enough, little noise. All are agreed that an eerie and appalling silence seemed to follow the salvo that blew the Hood to pieces.

If a shell had penetrated the deck near the mainmast, the nearest magazine would have been the 4-inch H.A. magazine, about sixty-five feet abaft the mast. The explosion of this magazine in itself might conceivably have caused the loss of the ship. It is more likely, though, that if it was the 4-inch magazine which went up, the ship was lost only because the 4-inch magazine set off the after 15-inch magazines. These contain 112 tons of cordite, and would have been sufficient to blow the bottom out of the ship. This would explain her terrifyingly sudden disappearance.

The three survivors were all conscious of the strange silence which seemed to descend upon the Hood after she was hit by the Bismarck's fifth salvo. Ordinary Signalman Briggs remembered the officer of the watch saying "The compass is gone" a few seconds before he himself was in the water. The compass in question would have been the gyro repeater-compass on the Hood's compass platform. The fact that it was suddenly "gone," or "dead," suggests a major hit which had possibly destroyed the ship's master gyro—located well below the water line. Able

Seaman Tilburn on the boatdeck remembered a tremendous vibration after the second hit, and a lot of gray smoke. The vibration was followed by a noise as if the Hood's guns had just fired (in fact, they had), and then a dead silence. Everyone on the bridge was thrown off his feet by the explosion. Only Midshipman Dundas, who climbed through one of the bridge windows as the ship tilted and sank, managed to escape. Like the other two survivors, he was also acutely conscious of the silence which followed the last explosion.

The Hood was still traveling fast through the water as she received her death blow. Within a few seconds the survivors found themselves swimming. They came to the surface close together, and reached some small rafts which had floated off the ship.

As the Hood heeled to port, broke in two, and sank, Lieutenant-Commander Terry of the Prince of Wales thought that he could see the ship's frames on the starboard side as she rolled over. The after part of the ship appeared to be a mass of twisted framework. Able Seaman Paton, also of the Prince of Wales, commented on seeing "jagged parts" of the Hood's stern. Then, her foretop fell backward, her stern slipped forward, and she was gone.

At the moment of the explosion, observers on the three other British ships saw giant fragments of the Hood in the air—part of the mainmast, the main derrick, a 15-inch gun, and even whole turrets. Able Seaman Tilburn reported that while he was in the water, he saw long tubes sealed at both ends floating near him. These, in all probability, would have been the crushing tubes from the bilges. The fact that these had been torn loose and blown to the surface confirms the magnitude of the damage. It suggests that the ship had broken her back.

It is likely that the hits obtained by the Bismarck's fifth salvo led to an explosion in the Hood's main after-magazines. Only the explosion of her 15-inch magazines could have caused such extensive and sudden damage. The Bismarck's shells had a muzzle velocity of 2,721 to 3,150 feet per second, and an expert's opinion is that if the Hood was struck by a shell with a muzzle velocity of over 3,050 f.p.s. it could have penetrated her main 12-inch armored belt and reached a magazine. Even if the shell had had a muzzle velocity of less than 2,721 f.p.s. it could have penetrated at one point on the ship's side—between the 12-inch belt and the flat section of the main protective deck. Yet a third possibility is that a shell with a fuse delay of about fifty-five feet, falling a fraction short of the ship, could, with its underwater travel, have entered the Hood below her armored belt.

The tragedy of the Hood is that at the moment when she was hit, she was executing the turn to port which would have enabled her broadsides to be brought to bear. The dangerous part of the run-in toward the enemy was over. Within minutes, or even seconds, the Vice-Admiral's two ships would have had the advantage of their greater firepower, and the action might well have ended in a very different way.

Envoi

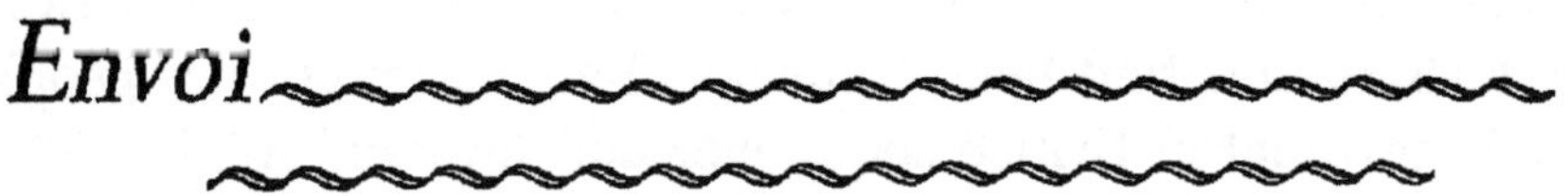

In 1694, George Savile, Marquis of Halifax, in a *Rough Draft of a New Model at Sea,* wrote:

"To the question, 'What shall we do to be saved in this world?' there is no other answer than this, 'Look to your Moat.' "

It was because the English people during the interwar years neglected their "Moat" that we entered World War II with a Navy, many of whose ships were, if not obsolete, at any rate obsolescent. The Hood was lost in the 1920's just as much as in the Denmark Strait in 1941. The defects in her design, to which attention had been called many years before, were never rectified. First of all, in the immediate postwar years, there had been the reluctance to spend large sums on capital ships. Secondly, the tide of events had caught up with her, so that it was never possible to take Britain's largest warship out of commission long enough to carry out the major alterations she required. For nearly a quarter of a century the Hood was the most famous ship in the world—a living legend. But one cannot make war with legends, and the fact remains that she was unable to withstand the punishment inflicted by 15-inch shells. *Capax imperii, nisi imperasset. . . .*

The greatest and most graceful ship of her time, perhaps of

any time, she was the last of the Leviathans—those mighty ships whose movements on the high seas had determined policy since the last quarter of the nineteenth century. A generation of British seamen had been trained in her. To millions of people she had represented British sea power and imperial might. With her passed not only a ship, but a whole era, swept away on the winds of the world.

APPENDIX A

OUTLINE OF THE HISTORY AND PRINCIPAL MOVEMENTS OF H.M.S. HOOD BETWEEN 1920 AND 1939

1920. May. The Hood, Tiger, and nine destroyers sailed on summer cruise to the Scandinavian countries. Hood did not visit Stockholm as her draft was too great. The King of Sweden and his son, Prince Eugen, visited her at Nynashamn. Rear-Admiral Sir Roger Keyes was in command of the squadron, flying his flag in the Hood. On conclusion of this cruise Hood returned to Scapa Flow.

1921. Cruise to Gibraltar and the Iberian Peninsula.

1922. Under flag of Rear-Admiral Sir Walter Cowan. Visited at Torbay by King George V. In September, together with the Repulse, sent to represent Great Britain at the celebrations in Brazil of the centenary of Brazilian independence. (At Rio de Janeiro Great Britain beat the United States in boxing match by four bouts to three. Five of the British boxers were members of the Hood's ship's company—three of them winning their fights.) The West Indies were visited. Torpedo and gunnery exercises carried out.

1923. Together with the Repulse and Snapdragon visited Norway and Denmark in June and July. November 27, in company with the Repulse and five ships from the First Light Cruiser Squadron (Delhi, Danae, Dragon, Dauntless, and Dunedin), Hood sailed on a round-the-world voyage. Object of this famous world tour was to visit parts of the Empire and provide a beneficent show of naval force in other areas. From Devonport the force proceeded to Sierra Leone, Cape Town, Durban, Zanzibar, Trincomalee, and Singapore.

1924. The end of the outward voyage, Melbourne, was reached on March 17, 1924. On the return journey the fleet visited Wellington, Auckland, Fiji, Honolulu, Vancouver, San Francisco, Panama, the West Indies, Halifax, and Quebec. The tour ended at Devonport on October 28, 1924, the force having steamed over 30,000 miles.

1925. In company with the Repulse visited Portugal (Lisbon) for the four hundredth anniversary of the great navigator Vasco da Gama.

1925–1927. Home Fleet, training and local cruises. Refit and repairs.

1928. Recommissioned under flag of Admiral Sir Frederick Dryer as flagship of the Battle Cruiser Squadron, Home Fleet.

1929–1930. Paid off into Dockyard Control at Portsmouth for extensive refit.

1931. The Hood recommissioned in March 1931 as an independent command. She joined the Atlantic Fleet.

1932. In company with the Repulse and the cruisers Delhi, Norfolk, and Dorsetshire she visited the West Indies. The fleet went first to Bridgetown, Barbados (January 21), then St. Vincent, Grenada, and finally Trinidad. In the summer the Hood visited Bangor and Guernsey, among other ports of the United Kingdom.

1933. Exercises in the Bay of Biscay and off Gibraltar. Visited Tangier together with the Renown. (The Admiral was congratulated by the local inspector of police on the excellent behavior of the British seamen.)

1934. Home Fleet.

1935. En route for Gibraltar from the West Indies a collision occurred between the Hood and Renown, Renown's bow striking Hood on the starboard side aft. Blades of starboard wing propeller were damaged as well as the starboard protection compartments. Repairs were carried out at Gibraltar and Portsmouth. There were no casualties. Later in the year Hood visited Las Palmas in the Canary Islands, Panama, and Funchal in the Madeiras on her return.

1936. Refit in August and then recommissioned for service with Mediterranean Fleet. The Spanish Civil War had broken out and Hood (flying the flag of Admiral Sir Geoffrey Blake) was sailed to assist in protecting British merchant shipping on the northern coast of Spain.

1937. In April the Thorpehall incident occurred—the S.S. Thorpehall, which had been previously declared free of war materials, being stopped outside territorial waters by Spanish insurgent ships. Hood and the Shropshire rendezvoused forty miles north of Bilbao to protect British interests.

1938. In January Hood sailed from Malta to Palma in Majorca. Vice-Admiral Commanding Battle Cruiser Squadron took over duties of senior officer commanding the Western Basin. Hood sailed for Barcelona on January 11 and thence to Valencia. During the major part of this year Hood was engaged in the western Mediterranean—Marseilles, Barcelona, and Palma. In an air raid on Palamos the British S.S. Lake Lugano was set on fire, the crew being taken on board Hood on August 9, 1938. Shortly after this, in company with the Sussex, she sailed from Palma to Malta, and thence to the United Kingdom.

1939. January to June: refitting and rearming. On completion, Hood joined the Home Fleet, her place in the Mediterrranean theater being taken by the Ramillies. Flag of Rear-Admiral Commanding Battle Cruiser Squadron was hoisted at Portsmouth June 1, 1939. From then until the outbreak of war Hood was working up and taking part in extensive trials with the Home Fleet.

APPENDIX B

SHIPS AND THEIR CAPTAINS FORMING THE SPECIAL SERVICE SQUADRON ENGAGED IN THE ROUND-THE-WORLD CRUISE OF 1923-24

Vice-Admiral Sir Frederick Laurence Field, K.C.B., C.M.G., in Command of the Squadron.

Rear-Admiral the Honorable Sir Hubert George Brand, K.C.M.G., K.C.V.O., C.B. Rear-Admiral Commanding First Light Cruiser Squadron.

H.M.S. Hood.	Captain J. K. Im Thurn, O.B.E.
H.M.S. Repulse.	Captain H. W. Parker, C.B.E.
H.M.S. Delhi.	Captain J. M. Pipon, M.V.O., O.B.E.
H.M.S. Dauntless.	Captain C. W. Round-Turner.
H.M.S. Danae.	Captain F. M. Austin.
H.M.S. Dragon.	Captain B. W. M. Fairbairn, C.B.E.
H.M.S. Dunedin.	Captain the Honorable A. R. M. Ramsay, D.S.O.

PEACE ESTABLISHMENT OF SHIP'S COMPANY IN 1923

Officers	70
Seamen	483
Boys	62
Marines	186
E/Room Estb.	302
Other nonexec. ratings	66
On world cruise	1,169

BOATS CARRIED

2	50-ft. steam pinnaces.	3	30-ft. gigs.
1	45-ft. steam barge.	2	27-ft. whalers.
1	35-ft. motorboat.	3	16-ft. dinghies.
1	42-ft. launch.	2	13½-ft. balsa rafts.
1	36-ft. pinnace.	4	patt. 18 carley floats.
4	32-ft. cutters.	2	patt. 19 carley floats.

2 patt. 20 carley floats.

APPENDIX C

CAPTAINS OF H.M.S. HOOD FROM 1920 TO 1941

1920	Captain W. Tomkinson.
1921–22	Captain G. Mackworth.
1923–24	Flag Captain J. K. Im Thurn.
1925–26	Flag Captain H. D. Reinold.
1927–28	Flag Captain W. F. French.
1929 1930	Lieutenant-Commander W. M. Phipps-Hornby. (Paid off into Dockyard Control, Portsmouth, 5/17/29) Lieutenant A. J. Mallett.
1931–32	Flag Captain J. F. C. Patterson.
1933	Flag Captain J. H. Binney.
1934–35	Flag Captain F. J. B. Tower.
1936–37	Flag Captain A. F. Pridham.
1938	Flag Captain H. T. C. Walker.
1939–40	Captain I. G. Glennie.
1941	Captain R. Kerr.

APPENDIX D

PRINCIPAL SHIPS INVOLVED IN THE BISMARCK ACTION

Features	BISMARCK	HOOD	RODNEY	KING GEORGE V	NORFOLK SUFFOLK DORSETSHIRE
Displacement (tons)	42,345 standard 52,700 fully loaded	42,462 standard (1941) 48,000 approx. fully loaded (1941)	33,900	35,000	10,000
Length	817′	860′	710′	746′	630′
Beam	118′	105′	106′	103′	66′
Draft	30′	28½′	30′	27.8′	17′
Complement	1,500	1,415	1,350	1,500	650
Launched	Feb. 1939	Aug. 1918	Dec. 1925	Feb. 1939	Jan. 1929
Completed	1940	1920	1927	1940	1930
Where built	Hamburg	Clyde	Liverpool	Newcastle	Portsmouth
Armament	8—15″ 12—5.9″ 16—4.1″	8—15″ 12—5.5″ 14—4″	9—16″ 12—6″ various A.A.	10—14″ 16—5.25″ various A.A.	8—8″ 8—4″ various A.A.
Speed—knots	30+	29.4 (1941)	22	30	30

BIBLIOGRAPHY

"Bismarck" (The Sinking of). Supplement to the *London Gazette,* No. 38098 (October 16, 1947).

Busch, Fritz Otto, *Das Geheimnis der Bismarck.* Hannover, A. Sponholtz, 1950.

Carver, Geoffrey, "Bismarck's End." *Life,* Vol. 1, No. 6 (1941).

Chalmers, William, *The Life and Letters of David, Earl Beatty.* London, Hodder and Stoughton, Ltd., 1951.

Churchill, Winston S., *The Second World War,* Vols. 1 and 2, *The Gathering Storm* and *Their Finest Hour.* Boston, Houghton Mifflin Company, 1948, 1949.

Cunningham, Andrew B., *A Sailor's Odyssey.* New York, E. P. Dutton and Company, Inc., 1951.

Fuehrer Conferences on Naval Affairs, 1944. British Admiralty, 1947.

Grenfell, Russell, *The Bismarck Episode.* New York, The Macmillan Company, 1949.

"H.M.S. Hood and After" and "The Value of Speed in Capital Ships." *Naval Review,* Vol. 8, No. 2 (1920).

Hinsley, Francis H., *Command of the Sea.* London, Christophers, Ltd., 1950.

James, William M., *The British Navies in the Second World War.* New York, Longmans, Green and Company, 1947.

Jameson, William S., *Ark Royal.* London, Rupert Hart-Davis, Ltd., 1957.

McMurtrie, Francis E., *The Cruise of the Bismarck.* London, Hutchinson and Company, Ltd., 1941.

Martienssen, Anthony K., *Hitler and His Admirals.* New York, E. P. Dutton and Company, Inc., 1949.

Parkes, Oscar, *British Battleships.* London, Seeley, Service and Company, Ltd., 1957.

Richmond, Herbert W., "Sea Warfare," in George Aston, ed., *The Study of War for Statesmen and Citizens.* New York, Longmans, Green and Company, 1933.

Roskill, Stephen W., "The War at Sea," in J. R. M. Butler, ed., *History of the Second World War,* Vol. 1. London, Her Majesty's Stationery Office, 1954-56.

——— *H.M.S. Warspite.* London, William Collins Sons and Company, Ltd., 1957.

Russell, Herbert W., *Ark Royal.* London, John Lane, The Bodley Head, Ltd., 1942.

Trogoff, Jean, *La Tragique Odysée du Cuirassé Bismarck.* Edition Ouest-France, 1953.

Tunstall, William, *World War at Sea.* London, Secker and Warburg, Ltd., 1942.

Varillon, Pierre, *Mers-el-Kebir.* Paris, Amiot-Dumont, 1949.

Vulliez, Albert, and Mordal, Jacques, *Battleship Scharnhorst,* trans. George Malcolm. London, Hutchinson and Company, Ltd., 1958.

The War, No. 38 (August 12, 1940).

Woodward, Ernest L., *Great Britain and the German Navy.* New York, Oxford University Press, 1935.

INDEX

(The ranks used in every case are those appertaining at the time.)

Abdiel (minelayer), 150
Achates (destroyer), 18, 160, 176-177
Adelaide, visit to, 81-83, 84
Adelaide (Australian cruiser), 86-87, 93
Admiralty, 20; standard practice against torpedo attack, 28-30, 46; regulation uniform, 57-58; joins consultation on world cruise, 69, 109-10, 119; regulations on ammunition storing, 124; creates Force H, 125; French fleet, 127-128, 129, 131-32; Italian fleet, 137-38; *Scheer's* movements undetected by, 144; diverts shipping in Atlantic, 145; pilot, 146; protection of Atlantic convoys, 150; pursuit of *Bismarck*, 160, 162, 184-185, 197, 198, 200-1; loss of *Hood*, communiqué, 195; Fighting Instructions, 212
Albany, visit to, 82
Alexandria, 128, 138, 140, 142, 149
Almirante Cervera (Spanish cruiser), 101-3
America, visit to, 89-92
Anglo-German Naval Treaty, 100
Anglo-Japanese Alliance, 48, 49
Antelope (destroyer), 18, 160, 176-177
Anthony (destroyer), 18, 160, 176-177
Apia, visit to, 89
Arethusa (light cruiser), 127, 163, 166
Argus (aircraft carrier), 142-43
Ark Royal (aircraft carrier), first bombing, 115; part of Force H, 125, 127, 184; Mers-el-Kebir, 128, 133; raid on Cagliari, 136, 137, 142; main objective of Italian bombers, 139, 141; pursuit of *Bismarck*, 202, 203-5
Armor plating, 25, 30-31, 42, 62-63, 110
Atlantic, Battle of the, 150-208
Atlantis (German ship), 167
Aurora (Canadian cruiser), 93, 166
Australia, visit to, 80-87; participation in Empire defense, 86-87
Australian Worker, 85

Balfour, Mr., 45, 47
Barbados, peacetime cruise to, 97-98
Battleships, 21-22, 32-33; *King George V* class, 151
Beatty, Admiral, 20, 26, 27, 28, 29, 35, 45, 48, 50, 114
Beaverbrook, Lord, 43
Belchen (German oil tanker), 155
Bergen, 144, 157, 158-59, 162, 163, 165, 171, 201, 202
Berry, William J., 32-33
Bilbao, blockade, 101-3
Birmingham (cruiser), 164, 166
Bismarck, world's most modern battleship, 16; nearing completion, 112; plan of escape into Atlantic, 144; trials and working up, 150; displacement, armament, and speed, 151-52; a fighting machine, 152; threat of raider foray, 153; on Operation RHEINUEBUNG, 155-

157; identified near Bergen, 158; possible breakout, 160; slips out from Bergen, 161; comparison with British battle cruisers, 162; heads for Arctic Circle, 166; route into Atlantic confirmed, 167-68; in Denmark Strait, 168; seen by *Suffolk*, 174; pursuit of, 175-89; battle with *Hood*, 190-94; sinks *Hood*, 193-94; continued pursuit of, 195-205; attacked, 205-7; sunk, 207; analysis of *Hood* battle, 210-219
Blake, Admiral Sir Geoffrey, 101, 102-3
Bluecher (German heavy cruiser), 112
Bowers, Claude G., 101
Brand, Rear-Admiral Sir Hubert, 70
Brazil, visit to, 61-68
Bretagne (French battleship), 128, 133
Briggs, Ordinary Signalman A. E., 196, 215, 216, 217
Briggs, Pilot Officer D. A., 201-2
Brown, John, and Company, 21

Cagliari, 136, 140, 142
Calabria, action off, 138, 140
Cape Times, 75
Capital ships, 32, 33, 41, 42, 46-47, 69, 73, 109, 121, 183, 185, 189, 220
Canada, visit to, 93-94
Chatfield, Admiral Sir Ernle, 28, 46, 48, 50
Churchill, Winston, 21; opinion of battle cruisers, 22; argument for fast battleships, 22; attitude toward war, 28, 100, 122-23
Coastal Command, 117, 163, 201-2
Colorado (American battleship), 83-84
Commandant Teste (French seaplane carrier), 128
Coode, Lieutenant-Commander T. P., 204
Copenhagen, visit to, 35
Cossack (destroyer), 147, 203
Cowan, Rear-Admiral Sir Walter, 68
Crete, 149, 156
Cruisers, 21-22, 46, 47; shortage of, 150; battle cruisers, 21, 22, 29-31, 108; First Battle Cruiser Squadron, 114; Second Battle Cruiser Squadron, 20, 114, 115, 198-99; Third Battle Cruiser Squadron, 26, 27; Eighteenth Cruiser Squadron, 115; First Light Cruiser Squadron, 70, 71, 72, 73-74, 75-76, 77, 82, 86-87, 92, 94; *Dido* class, 109-10
Cruises, peacetime, Mediterranean, 38-44; Brazil, 61-68; world, 69-94; press reports on, 74, 75, 80-84, 90, 91, 93-94; West Indian, 97-98
Cunningham, Admiral, 41, 128, 136, 139, 140-41, 142, 149

Dalrymple-Hamilton, Captain, 201, 206-7
Denmark Strait, mentioned, 19, 24, 43; *Bismarck's* escape route, 144, 155, 157-59, 161, 166; H.M.S. *Suffolk* and *Norfolk* in, 166, 172, 173; conditions in, 167-70, 171; *Bismarck* sighted in, 175-77, 183; pursuit of *Bismarck* in, 180-81, 185, 199-200, 203-4; *Hood* sunk in, 194, 220
Destroyer Flotilla, Fourth, 203
Devonport, 124
Dogger Bank, 114-15
Dorsetshire (cruiser), 97, 127, 207
Dryer, Admiral Sir Frederick, 96
Dundas, Midshipman W. J., 196, 215, 216, 218
Dunedin (light cruiser), 70, 87
Dunkerque (French battle cruiser), 119, 120, 128, 130, 131, 132, 133
Dunkirk, 125
Durban, visit to, 77

Echo (destroyer), 18, 147, 160, 176-177
Eden, Sir Anthony, 100-1
Electra (destroyer), 18, 147, 160, 176-77

Ellis, Captain R. M., 172, 174
Enterprise (light cruiser), 127, 142
Esmonde, Lieutenant-Commander E., 199

Faeroe Islands, 113, 119, 145, 157, 158, 173
Fancourt, Captain H. St. J, 163
Fegen, Captain E. S. F., 145
Field, Vice-Admiral Sir Frederic Laurence, in command of world cruise, 70, 71; as ambassador, 71-72, 74; received by Sultan of Zanzibar, 78; parries criticism of Singapore's naval base, 80; interviewed by Australian press, 81-82; successful visit to Australia, 84-85; tact of, 89-90; popularity of, 90; passage through Panama Canal, 92; on Canada's naval defense, 93-94
Fiji Islands, visit to, 87-89
Fisher, Lord, 20-21
Fleet, British, 16, 130, 138, 155, 158, 194; Admirals of, 32; Air Arm, 202, 205; Grand, 26, 29, 154
Forbes, Admiral, 115, 117, 121, 122
Force H, 125, 127, 128, 130, 131, 132, 134, 135-36, 140, 141, 142-143, 145-46, 184, 198, 201
Four Power Pacific Treaty, 49
Foxhound (destroyer), 128-29, 130
Franco, 100, 102
Fremantle, visit to, 77, 80
French fleet, 127, 128, 129, 130, 131, 132, 133, 134; Armistice, 129, 132; *Force de Raid*, 120

Galatea (cruiser), 166, 178
Galerna (Spanish armed trawler), 101, 102
Geddes, Sir Auckland, 45
Geddes, Sir Eric, 43-44, 49; "Geddes Ax," 44
General Messing System, 54
Gensoul, Vice-Admiral, 119, 128-29, 130-34
George V, H.M. King, 70, 71
Germany, High Seas Fleet, 21, 24, 26, 29, 35; pocket battleships, 100, 112; fleet, 111-12, 117; U-boats, 100, 112, 149, 150; Naval Planning Staff, 119, 156; Admiralty, 144, 155, 200, 214; forces sweep Europe, 149; *Luftwaffe*, 138, 149; Operation RHEINUEBUNG, 155-57, 198, 200; Third Reich, 149, 156; vessels, similarity of, 184
Gibraltar, 36, 37, 39, 125, 126-27, 134, 135, 138, 140, 142, 162, 163, 184, 198
Gick, Lieutenant P., R.N., 199
Glennie, Captain I. G., 159
Gloucester (cruiser), 139
Gneisenau (German battle cruiser), 112, 116-17, 119, 128, 150, 156, 183
Goddard, Lieutenant N. N., R.N.-V.R., 165
Graf Spee (German pocket battleship), 118-19
Gunnery, of British fleet, 29, 73, 104-7; efficiency of German, 176, 197, 205
Guns, on the *Dreadnought*, 21; weight on ships, 21-22; on the *Hood*, 25, 43, 63, 104-13, 124, 139; antiaircraft, 63, 96-97, 109

Hammocks, 52-53
Hamsterley (British merchant ship), 102-3
Harding, President, 45
Hatston, Royal Naval Air Station, 163, 165
Hermione (cruiser), 163, 166
Hinsley, F. H., 45
Hipper (German cruiser), 112, 144, 150; *Hipper* class cruisers, 158
Hitler, Adolf, 112, 200, 205-6; his *Blitzkrieg*, 142
Hobart, Tasmania, visit to, 86
Holland, Captain C. S., 129, 130-31, 132, 134
Holland, Vice-Admiral L. E., C.B., Second-in-Command, Home Fleet, 19, 159, 160; pursuit of *Bismarck*,

161, 166, 170, 173, 175, 176-77, 178; loses contact with *Suffolk*, 180; alters squadron's course, 182-183; policy of radar silence, 183; does not recall destroyers, 185; race to intercept *Bismarck*, 187-188; battle tactics against *Bismarck*, 189-93; loss of *Hood*, 195; analysis of *Bismarck* action, 210-214, 216-17, 219

Home Fleet, 95-96, 114, 115, 117, 118, 119, 121, 150, 157, 159, 171, 189; principal war base, 122, 181; Commander-in-Chief, 145, 153, 157-59, 188-89

Honolulu, visit to, 89-90

Hood (battle cruiser), leaves Scapa Flow, 17-18; length, 18, 83; displacement, 18, 24, 92, 111, 118, 151; laid down, 21, designed as battle cruiser, 21; ancestry, 22; launching, 23, 27; design and requirements, 23-24; disadvantages, 24; speed, 24, 41, 42, 120, 137; cost, 24, 85, 99; construction, 25, armor, 24, 25, 50, 110; armor plating, 25, 42, role in politics, 26, 31, 33-34, 220-21; name, 26-27; crest, 26; range in battle, 30, 189-90, 191, 192, 211-13; defects in design, 30-31, 220; commissioned, 32; last voyage, 34; first voyage, 34; sinking of, mentioned, 36; Mediterranean cruise, 36-44; a boxing ship, 37; turbine engines, 43; propellers, 43; searchlights, 43; effect of Washington Treaty on, 50; life on board, 51-60, 64-67; complement, 51, 113; visits Brazil, 61-62, 67-68; a wet ship aft, 62, 111; guns of, 62-63, 104-111, 123-24; antiaircraft defense, 63, 110, 111, 124; prayers, 64; chapel, 64; ventilation, 64-65; world cruise, 69-94; calls at Freetown, 71, 72; good behavior of sailors, 72, 75, 86; visits Zanzibar, 77-78; reception in Australia, 80-86; own motor transport, 80; spaciousness of, 81; dimensions of, 83-84; visits New Zealand, 87; visits Fiji, 87-89; first visit to America, 89-90; in San Francisco Harbor, 91-92; passage through Panama Canal, 92; visits Jamaica, 92-93; calls at Halifax, 93-94; rejoins Home Fleet, 95; visits Lisbon, 95-96; first major refit, 96; West Indian cruise, 97-98; involved in Spanish Civil War, 100-103; duties in Western Mediterranean, 103; in World War II, 114-219; North Sea patrol, 114-121; bombing of, 116; kernel of Force H, 125; at Mers-el-Kebir, 128-34; Mediterranean 1940, 135-143; bombed by Italian Air Force, 138-40; Operation HURRY, 142-143; covers Northern approaches, 145-47; fitted with gunnery radar, 154; in Battle of Atlantic, 154-94; in pursuit of *Bismarck*, 160-86; battle with *Bismarck*, 187-94; sinking of, 193-94; loss reported, 196, 198; survivors from, 196, 215-218; analysis of *Bismarck* battle, 210-19

Hood, Lady, 23, 27

Hood, Rear-Admiral Hon. Horace Lambert, 26, 27, 30

Hood, Viscount Samuel, 26

Icarus (destroyer), 18, 160, 176

Iceland-Faeroes channel, 157, 163, 166, 172, 173; patrol, 171-72, 200

Indefatigable (battle cruiser), 31

Invincible (battle cruiser), 26, 27, 31

Italian, Navy, 99-100; fleet, 136, 137-38, 140, 149; Air Force, 138-139, 141-42

Japan, 45, 46, 48, 49, 79

Jellicoe, Admiral, 16, 28-29, 30, 154

Jervis Bay (armed merchant cruiser), 144, 145

Jutland, Battle of, 18, 24, 25, 26-27, 28, 29, 30, 31, 42, 106, 210

Kennedy, Captain E. C., 119
Kenya, 166
Kerr, Captain R., 159, 194
Keyes, Vice-Admiral Sir Roger, 35
King George V (battleship), 157, 159, 162, 176, 180, 193, 197, 200, 202, 206, 207, 214
Kirchberg, Leading Seaman, 199
Köln (German heavy cruiser), 117

Larcom, Captain, 203
Leach, Captain, 191, 194, 217
Lend-Lease Bill, 150
Lion (battle cruiser), 27, 28
Lisbon, visit to, 95-96
Loch Ewe, 117, 121
London Naval Conference, 50, 100
Lutjens, Vice-Admiral, in command Operation RHEINUEBUNG, 156, 157; helped by weather, 161, 171, 201; heads toward Arctic, 166; bent on escape, 177; eludes *Suffolk*, 180, 183; unaware of capital ships, 184-85, 188-89; sights *Hood*, 191; in action against *Hood*, 191-93; confusion between *Prince of Wales* and *Hood*, 193, 214; abandons Atlantic raid, 197-98; and British radar, 200; speech to crew, 204; *Bismarck* hit, 205

Macgregor (merchant ship), 102-3
Malta, 136, 138, 142, 143, 149
Manchester (cruiser), 163, 166
Manthey, Ordinary Seaman, 205, 214
Maori (destroyer), 203
Marschall, Admiral, 119
Matapan, 138
Mediterranean, 33; cruise, 36-44; duties in, 103, 109, 126-43, 149, 181; Fleet, 136, 138-39, 141, 142
Melbourne, visit to, 81-83, 84-85, 86
Mers-el-Kebir, 128-34
Modoc (U. S. Coast Guard cutter), 199
Mopan (merchant ship), 144
Mussolini, Benito, 39

Naval Review, 24, 42
Nelson (battleship), 18, 46, 115, 117-18, 120-21
Newcastle (cruiser), 119
Newell, Able Seaman, 174, 202
New York *Herald Tribune*, 91
New Zealand, visit to, 87
Nonintervention, policy of, 100-1
Norfolk (cruiser), escort to Barbados, 97; Denmark Strait patrol, 159, 166, 168, 170, 172, 173; shadows *Bismarck*, 174-75, 177, 178, 188-90; under *Bismarck's* fire, 176; mentioned, 182, 184, 196; to concentrate on *Prinz Eugen*, 191; watches *Hood-Bismarck* battle, 192; pursues *Bismarck*, 198-199, 200; account of *Hood-Bismarck* action, 214, 215
North, Admiral Sir Dudley, 126
Norway, visit to, 35, 149, 150, 156, 158, 159, 166; Allied Expeditionary Force to, 124

Oran, 128, 130
Operation CATAPULT, 128-34
Operation HURRY, 142

Panama Canal Record, 92
Pax Britannica, 45
Perth, Australia, visit to, 83
Phillips, Captain A. J. L., 174-75, 176, 215
Piorun (Polish destroyer), 203
Polish Navy, 203
Port Royal, Jamaica, visit to, 92
Press, 32, 47, 79, 80; world cruise reports, Afrikaans, 74, 75; Australian, 83-84, 85; British Labour, 94
Prien, Lieutenant Gunther, 16-17
Prince of Wales (battleship), leaves Scapa Flow, 17; covers northern approaches, 159-60, 166, 173; new ship, 162; pursuit of *Bismarck*, 175-176, 178-79, 180, 181, 182-84, 185-86, 187-88, 190; engages *Bismarck*, 191-94; and sinking of *Hood*, 193-94; damaged, 196; de-

fects of, 197; and *Bismarck*, 199, 200; analysis of action, 210-18
Prinz Eugen (German heavy cruiser), at sea with *Bismarck*, 16; and German fleet, 112; completed, 150; description of, 152-53; raider foray, 153; damaged, 155; to destroy merchantmen, 155; escape from North Sea, 156-57; identified near Bergen, 158; mentioned, 167, heads for Denmark Strait, 170; sighted by *Suffolk*, 174; in Denmark Strait, 175-76, 177; pursuit of, 181, 188-89; similarity to *Bismarck*, 184; damages *Prince of Wales*, 196; detached from *Bismarck*, 198; analysis of *Hood-Bismarck* action, 210, 213, 214
Provence (French battleship), 128, 133

Queen Mary (battle cruiser), 28, 31

Radar, 43, 74, 105, 154, 172, 173, 178, 180, 183, 199, 200, 202, 213
Raeder, Admiral, 111, 156; his Z plan, 112
Ramillies (battleship), 184, 197
Rawalpindi (armed merchant cruiser), 119
Renown (battle cruiser), 113, 123, 143, 184, 202
Repulse (battle cruiser), 70, 75, 82, 92, 97, 98, 115, 117, 123, 145, 162, 166
Resolution (battleship), 128, 135
Revenge (battleship), 184
Reykjanes, 146, 173
Riccardi, Admiral, 141
Richelieu (French battleship), 127
Rio de Janeiro, visit to, 37, 64, 67-68
Rodney (battleship), 18, 46, 115, 117-18, 121, 122-23, 184, 197, 201, 202, 204, 206-7
Roskill, Captain S. W., 128
Rotherham, Commander G. A., R.N., 165
Royal Navy, 24, 44, 49-50, 69, 74, 101, 111, 112-13, 127, 130, 133, 196
Royal Oak (battleship), 16, 120
Rum issue, 53-54

San Francisco, visit to, 90-92; tribute to *Hood*, 91
Sayid Khalifa Ben Hamid, Sultan of Zanzibar, 78
Scapa Flow, 15-17, 18-19, 34-35, 113, 120, 122-23, 145, 146, 157, 158, 161, 162, 163, 171
Scharnhorst (German battle cruiser), 112, 119, 128, 145, 150, 156, 183
Scheer, Admiral (German pocket battleship), 112, 144, 146, 167
Schneider, Lieut.-Commander, 205
Sea power, 31, 33, 75, 85, 112, 221
Sheffield (cruiser), 184, 203, 204
Shipping losses, 16, 30, 31, 106, 149-150, 153
Shropshire (cruiser), 101
Sierra Leone, visit to, 71, 125
Sikh (destroyer), 203
Singapore, visit to, 79; criticism of naval base at, 80
Skagerrak, 117, 119
Slang, sailors', 54-56, 57
Somerville, Vice-Admiral Sir James, 125, 127, 128, 129, 130, 132, 134, 142, 143, 184, 198
Spanish Civil War, policy of non-intervention, 100-1; bombing of British merchant ships, 101-2; Bilbao blockade, 101-3
Spearfish (submarine), 115
Stanbrook (merchant ship), 102-3
Steer, G. L., 102-3
Strasbourg (French battle cruiser), 128, 133
Suffolk (cruiser), described, 152-53; rejoins *Norfolk* in Denmark Strait, 159, 166, 168, 170, 172, 173; sights *Bismarck*, 174; shadows *Bismarck*, 174-75, 177-78, 188-89; loses radar contact, 180-81, 182; concentrates on *Prinz Eugen*, 191; watches *Hood-Bismarck* action,

192; pursuit of *Bismarck,* 198, 200; analysis of *Hood-Bismarck* action, 214

Ten-Year Rule, 49-50
Thorpehall incident, 101-3
Tiger (battle cruiser), 35, 38
Tilburn, Able Seaman R. E., 196, 215, 218
Tirpitz, Admiral Alfred von, 31, 151
Tirpitz (German battleship), 112, 151, 155, 185
Topsail Bay, Newfoundland, visit to, 94
Torpedoes, *Hood's*, 25; attack by, 28-29; threat to sea power, 31
Toulon, 43, 133
Tovey, Admiral Sir John, and threat of *Bismarck,* 151, 153; *Bismarck,* 157-58, 159, 160, 161-63, 165, 166, 167, 176, 178, 183, 185; hampered by weather, 171; lack of news, 173, 175, 180; pursuit of *Bismarck,* 197, 198, 200-1, 202, 204; attack on *Bismarck,* 206-7; analysis of *Hood-Bismarck* action, 212
Trincomalee, visit to, 79

Uniform, naval, 57-58
Unrotated projectile equipment, 124, 216

Valiant (battleship), 122, 127
Vian, Captain P. L., D.S.O., 203, 204
Victorious (aircraft carrier), 162, 163, 166, 173, 197, 198, 199*n.*

Wake-Walker, Rear-Admiral W. F., 172, 196, 197
Warspite (battleship), 140
Washington Conference, 44-49
Washington ships, 46, 118
Washington Treaty, 44, 47-48, 49, 50, 111, 151, 152
Wellington, New Zealand, visit to, 87
Wells, Vice-Admiral L. V., 126
Whitworth, Vice-Admiral W. J., 114, 117, 119, 159
World Crisis, The, 1911-14, 22
World War I, 20-21, 25, 26, 106, 112, 114-15, 151, 152, 154
World War II, 15-19, 31, 33, 43, 46, 49, 80, 97, 99, 114-219, 220; Cabinet, 128, 153

Zanzibar, visit to, 77-78
Zulu (destroyer), 203

This book was set in
Caledonia and Perpetua types,
printed, and bound by
The Haddon Craftsmen.
It was designed by
Larry Kamp.

Lightning Source UK Ltd.
Milton Keynes UK
UKHW050916150822
407319UK00008B/1519